D1304849

Truth and Rumors

Truth and Rumors

The Reality Behind
TV's Most Famous Myths

BILL BRIOUX

The Praeger Television Collection
David Bianculli, Series Editor

PRAEGER

Westport, Connecticut
London

Library of Congress Cataloging-in-Publication Data

Brioux, Bill.
    Truth and rumors : the reality behind TV's most famous myths / Bill Brioux.
            p. cm. — (The Praeger television collection, ISSN 1549-2257)
    Includes bibliographical references and index.
    ISBN 978-0-275-99247-7 (hardcover: alk. paper)
1. Television broadcasting—United States—Miscellanea. I. Title.
PN1992.3.U5B75   2008
791.450973—dc22   2007037547

British Library Cataloguing in Publication Data is available.

Library of Congress Catalog Card Number: 2007037547
ISBN: 978-0-275-99247-7
ISSN: 1549-2257

First published in 2008

Praeger Publishers, 88 Post Road West, Westport, CT 06881
An imprint of Greenwood Publishing Group, Inc.
www.praeger.com

Printed in the United States of America

The paper used in this book complies with the
Permanent Paper Standard issued by the National
Information Standards Organization (Z39.48–1984).

10 9 8 7 6 5 4 3 2 1

To my parents,
Margaret and Ross,
for raising me right—in front of the television.

Contents

Acknowledgments

Did you know that writing a book is roughly the equivalent of writing 100 daily newspaper columns? I know, big deal, there's still no heavy lifting. As they would say on *Seinfeld*, "Yadda, yadda, yadda."

Still, sorting through 60 years of broadcasting truths and rumors involves a great deal of research and fact checking, and I am indebted to several people for helping me with those tasks. Former colleague Janet Rowe, who I worked with several years ago at *TV Guide* Canada, graciously offered to track down some key articles in the old *TV Guide* research department stacks. The librarians at the Toronto, Mississauga and Brampton, Ontario, Public Libraries, as well as the Ryerson University library staff, were all very helpful and efficient. If I sell enough copies of this book, maybe one day I can pay off all my library fines.

A debt is owed to The Paley Center for Media (formerly the Museum of Television and Radio), both in New York and Los Angeles, where, over the years, I screened several of the programs discussed in this book. Their vast collections are a valuable resource in verifying some TV legends and debunking others.

Former *Toronto Sun* entertainment editor Kathy Brooks, the best copy editor I ever worked for, gave this entire manuscript a once over. There is no greater assurance for a writer than her set of eyes, and few rewards greater than making them dance.

Fred Wostbrook, author of *The Ultimate TV Game Show Book* and agent to many of the stars of TV's golden era, graciously helped connect me with a few of the key voices for this book.

Truth and Rumors would not have been possible without the Television Critics Association's (TCA) semiannual network press tour. Many of these stories were collected and banked while attending TCA tour sessions over the past 20 years. For a reporter, especially one from Canada, there is no greater access anywhere to TV's movers and shakers.

It was a colorful colleague on the TCA board of directors, *New York Daily News* TV columnist David Bianculli, who got this whole thing started by asking, "Ever thought of writing a book about television?" This is what happens when you hang around TV critics who wear Hawaiian shirts.

Finally, thanks to Daniel Harmon, my editor at Praeger, for being the most patient man in publishing. This book was started so long ago, Abe Vigoda was still dead!

Introduction

When people first heard it, they couldn't believe it: Jerry Mathers, the freckle-faced little tyke who played adorable Theodore "Beaver" Cleaver on *Leave It to Beaver*, was dead.

The rumor quickly spread throughout North America that he had been killed in Vietnam.

Turns out there was a good reason to be skeptical: it wasn't true. Trouble is, there are still people to this day who insist Mathers is dead, even when he denies it to their face.

It doesn't stop there. For years, people have been convinced that Abe Vigoda, the actor who played curmudgeonly cop Fish on *Barney Miller*, is dead. People swear he has passed on, no matter how many times he appears decked out like a Christmas tree on *Late Night with Conan O'Brien*. Or that Mikey, the kid who would eat anything as the Life cereal tyke, had eaten too many Pop Rocks and exploded. Or—and this is one everybody is sure they heard—that a contestant on *The Newlywed Game* once said the strangest place they ever made "whoopee" was "in the butt, Bob."

By the '90s, people were certain that Steve, the dude who appeared in the animated kiddie show *Blue's Clues*, had died of a heroin overdose. Or that watching *Sailor Moon* caused convulsions. Or that Josh Saviano, Kevin's geeky pal on *The Wonder Years*, had grown up to become Marilyn Manson.

It is still going on. Rumors persist that fashion designer Tommy Hilfiger made racist statements on *Oprah Winfrey*. Jared Fogle, the guy who lost all that weight eating Subway sandwiches, choked on one and died. One of the dudes from *The Bachelor* got three contestants pregnant.

How did these and dozens of other TV-related rumors get started? How did they spread from classrooms to boardrooms across North America and sometimes beyond? How did they become so readily accepted as facts?

The answer, of course, is the incredible reach and persuasiveness of television. Besides exposing us to things we can't believe, it can convince us of things that never actually happened.

The universal shared experience of attending the funeral of John F. Kennedy, seeing The Beatles for the first time on *Ed Sullivan* or Neil Armstrong's step on the surface of the moon was historic and unprecedented. Even as TV viewing splintered with the arrival of hundreds of new channels, VCRs, and DVDs, millions still returned to share in the bizarre sight of a white Ford Bronco fleeing along a California highway or to witness the horrific destruction of the World Trade Center towers.

The dizzying highs and lows of those shared moments creates a "you are there" immediacy that no other medium can trigger. Is it any wonder, then, that similar urban legends and rumors grow out of those shared experiences?

People always want to be in the know, even if it never happened. And with so many bizarre occurrences unfolding on television—such as the O.J. Simpson, Robert Blake, and Michael Jackson trials—many urban myths seem more and more plausible.

An urban legend is basically a false truth that has taken root in people's imaginations and has stood the test of time. Then there are rumors, basically just unverified information that sounds tantalizingly real (and, in just enough cases to keep us keen, turn out to be true). While all the urban legends or rumors in this book originated through television, home computers and the Internet have added fuel to this wildfire, spreading rumors from home to home with an immediate, high speed intensity.

The purpose of this book isn't simply to debunk rumors or legends—what's the fun in that? I want to believe Frank Zappa's dad was Mr. Green Jeans (boomers will remember him as Captain Kangaroo's sidekick) as much as the next guy.

Instead, the idea here is to get to the truth behind the rumors, wherever possible, from the personalities involved. Some of their explanations turn out to be better than the rumors themselves. Some TV truths are even wilder than the rumors. And, in a few instances, some of those persistent rumors turn out to have actually occurred.

In a larger sense, this book springs from a curiosity about truth, lies, and television. TV is so persuasive it can make you believe things you never saw or heard. It can also convince you that things you actually witnessed never happened.

The rise of so-called reality television in the last decade has blurred the lines like never before. Shows like *Survivor* and *The Amazing Race* are cast, shot, and edited to heighten and exploit reality, not to capture it. Nobody wants to see 16 or 20 people just standing around. Even a voyeur needs a story, and the juicier the better.

These days, when people hear that original *Survivor* winner Richard Hatch never declared his million-dollar winnings and was convicted of tax evasion—a setup for an urban legend if there ever was one—they not only believe it, they somehow expect it.

Same with the original *Joe Millionaire*, Evan Marriott. Even though hunky Marriott was presented as a journeyman contractor posing as a wealthy playboy (and thus irresistible to the women vying for him on the outrageous dating series), many viewers were convinced that he was in fact rich all along, an heir to the Marriott Hotel chain fortune. Viewers have come to expect the unexpected from television. They are looking for the crazy twist that changes everything a the end—even if it never comes.

That certainly wasn't the case back in TV's—and my own—more innocent days. Back in the '50s and '60s, people tended to believe everything they saw on television. That was especially true before the quiz show scandals of the mid-50s. A lot of eyes were opened wide when Charles Van Doren, a clean-cut college lecturer who seemed like an unbeatable brainiac on a show called *Twenty-One*, finally came clean and admitted he was given answers beforehand. People were stunned and their faith in TV was shattered forever.

Almost as stunned as I was as a youngster by three things I swore I saw on TV. Did any of them really happen?

Like a lot of other young boomers, I spent way too much time in front of the TV. As an only child growing up in Toronto in the '60s, I spent countless hours in front of my parent's 19-inch, black-and-white Marconi.

Some of my earliest memories are of watching animated kiddie fare, such as Felix the Cat and his bag of tricks, those old Popeye cartoons with the slamming wooden ship door titles, the breezy banter of The Friendly Giant (a Canadian kiddie TV icon), and Sherri Lewis and her button-eyed sock puppet, Lambchop.

More than half of those images were beamed from nearby Buffalo, New York, where TV shows from ABC, CBS, and NBC affiliates flooded across the border. CBS's *Captain Kangaroo* was just as big a hit for Canadian preschoolers in the early '60s, for example, as it was in the States.

It was the local kiddie shows, however, that often had the most hypnotic impact. Usually hosted by the station's weatherman or a sportscaster who was picking up a few extra bucks doing double duty, they were bizarre, beyond low-budget, and totally devoid of educational values. In other words, they were irresistible to kids.

The way three of my favorite kiddie shows ended has haunted me all my life. But did they really end that way or did I imagine it?

One was a local, cheaply produced Canadian show called *Kiddo the Clown*. Kiddo was a typical circus clown, very much cut from the same ratty cloth as Ringling Brothers icon Emmett Kelly, with a painted-on smile, crushed hat, and a black greasepaint beard.

He lived in a dingy, underground lair. One day, construction workers smashed through one of his cave-like walls. The subway (which, in fact, was expanding in Toronto at that time) was being extended, and the proposed route ran right through Kiddo's underground abode. As the workers started laying down tracks, Kiddo was kicked out, and the show was kaput. G'bye, kids!

The second show was *Diver Dan*, a bizarre, syndicated series that originated out of Philadelphia. Diver Dan was a fairly nondescript dude (you could never really see his face under that large metal helmet with the tiny round window) who explored the seas in one of those deep-sea diving suits. His friends were Minerva, a long-haired mermaid, and a school of wooden puppet fish (including the villainous Baron Barracuda). In a lame attempt to make *Diver Dan* look like it took place under the sea, all the human and puppet characters were shot through a giant fish tank.

The shows only lasted 10 or 15 minutes each day. One morning, an episode ended with Dan wrapped in the tentacles of a giant squid. TV's first kiddie cliffhanger! The next morning, I could hardly wait to run to the set to see how my hero escaped. Except he didn't escape, as the announcer dryly informed me and many other wide-eyed youngsters. On screen was Dan's helmeted head, framed in a thick, black border. "Diver Dan," we were told, "had drowned and would not be back on the air." The end!

The third show was *Captain Bob*, or *Captain Sam*, or something like that. It was, I believe, from one of the New York stations. This station showed all the cool Popeye cartoons and was hosted by an actor playing the Captain who chatted with his first mate, a Popeye-like marionette.

The show was coming to the end of another day, when all of a sudden water started rapidly filling up on screen (again, the corny old shot through the fish tank gag). Apparently, the ship had struck a rock or iceberg or something and was sinking. The captain and the first mate went down with the ship, gurgling their hasty goodbyes. The show went off the air, never to return!

That kind of TV trauma stays with you when you are four.

Years later, when I started writing about television at the *Toronto Sun*, I chronicled these three bizarre stories. Did anybody else out there see them? Was I daydreaming at the time or did all three end the way I remembered them ending?

To my surprise, Kiddo came clean. Trevor Evans, an actor who had played Kiddo the Clown and who had gone on to a directing career, saw my story in the paper and dropped in at the newspaper, bringing with him an autographed photo of Kiddo.

Yes, the series, which ran in 1962, ended with Kiddo being booted out of his cave by track-laying construction workers. Evans told me he was being paid peanuts at the time and that he had gone in to see his bosses, demanding a raise. The suits at the station told him to quit clowning and get back to work or be fired. The subway sendoff was his peeved revenge. Kiddo was kaput, but Evans found a way to have the last laugh—even if he did mess with a few young heads.

I never did get any feedback about the other two endings. But in checking out the many urban legends examined in this book, I've discovered that one real story, or even a whiff of truth, can lead to several copycat stories. All it takes is for one child star to meet a sad end for several other actors to go through the rest of their lives saying, "No, I'm still alive, you must be thinking of the freckle-faced kid in pigtails from *Family Affair*."

What follows, then, are over 150 of TV's most enduring legends, rumors, and urban myths. In over 20 years on the TV beat, I've asked everyone from Henry Winkler (*Happy Days'* the Fonz) to William Shatner (*Star Trek's* Captain Kirk), from Micky Dolenz (*The Monkees*) to David Cassidy (*The Partridge Family*), and from '50s pioneers Art Linkletter and Milton Berle to today's *Survivor* and *Amazing Race* contestants about the rumors associated with their shows. Whether they turn out to be true, false, or, in some cases, unsubstantiated, their answers may surprise you. As Mark Twain once said, "Truth is stranger than fiction, but it is because fiction is obliged to stick to possibilities; truth isn't."

CHAPTER 1

How False Was It? The Show That Spawned the Most Myths: *The Tonight Show Starring Johnny Carson*

The *Tonight Show Starring Johnny Carson* was the "late night place to be" when it came to rumors, legends, and urban myths on television.

Carson, a nimble-witted Nebraska native who died in January of 2005, was TV's original brat. His blend of sophistication and silliness made him the perfect late night host during the ever-more permissive '60s and '70s.

Back then, an average audience of eight million Americans went to bed with Carson every night. *The Tonight Show* was a love-in, and Carson was the sly and sanitized Hugh Hefner of the airwaves.

The Tonight Show Starring Johnny Carson ran for 30 uninterrupted years, from 1962 to 1992. The extraordinary longevity of the series and of Carson as host simply added to its legend. After 5,000 shows, you'd expect a few whoppers to emerge and myths to stick.

Carson's offscreen elusiveness also added to his cultish fascination. Despite being the King of Late Night, Carson was rarely spotted in prime time or in other media, and all but vanished upon retiring in 1992. He seldom granted interviews, and when he did, reporters—even the legendary *60 Minutes* team—came away frustrated. *Playboy* described him in 1967 as "paradoxical." We knew him, but we never really knew him.

In *Glued to the Set: The 60 Television Shows and Events That Made Us Who We Are Today*, author Steven D. Stark pointed out that midnight man Carson was the most familiar voice we heard as we drifted between wakefulness and sleep. "Ordinary yet dislocated, relevant yet forgettable," wrote Stark, "Carson's show served as a bridge between our tangible world and the world of our dreams." No wonder then, that we sometimes ask ourselves, did Johnny really say or do all those things, or did we simply dream it?

That question is a big reason for Carson's *Tonight Show* spreading more urban myths and rumors than all the other talk shows put together. But there is another reason: lack of evidence to the contrary.

In a short-sighted move, designed at the time to save money, NBC bulk erased thousands of *Tonight Show* tapes stored in a New York warehouse. The tapes were recycled, with new episodes taped over the old ones.

Lost were nearly all of Jack Paar's five year tenure on *The Tonight Show* (for some reason, only the Friday episodes were kept), plus the first 10 Carson years, from 1962 to '72. Gone, among many other moments, is Carson's very first show as host, plus the 1968 *Tonight Show* appearance of Beatles John Lennon and Paul McCartney. What survives from this era are just a few Telecine 16mm prints in personal collections, some clips that had already been pulled for anniversary episodes, and a few other films released in edited form for the Armed Forces Network (including the memorable 1969 moment when George Gobel, who had to follow surprise guests Bob Hope and Dean Martin, quipped, "Did you ever get the feeling that the world was a tuxedo and you were a pair of brown shoes?").

The loss of a decade of *Tonight Show* tapes makes it difficult to completely deny several Internet rumors—and that much easier for them to spread unchecked. Among the whoppers:

RUMOR: *Frequent* Tonight Show *guest Zsa Zsa Gabor once sat on Carson's couch with her Persian cat on her lap. She asked the host if he wanted to pet her pussy. To which Carson replied, "Yeah, but the damn cat's in the way."*

FALSE: *The urban-legends debunking Internet site Snopes.com calls this "the greatest manufactured memory in modern culture." In some versions of this story, Raquel Welch, Ann-Margret, Dyan Cannon, Farrah Fawcett-Majors, or Jane Fonda is substituted for Gabor. That alone makes this a little fishy—it's almost as if the star changes to suit the times as this rumor is being passed along.*

Both Gabor and Carson repeatedly denied it. Letters from each of them shooting down the rumor appear on the Snopes.com Web site. Gabor's letter, written in August of 1996, simply says, "The incident to which you are reffering [sic] never happened." Carson's letter, dated later the same year, states, "I rather wish it had happened because it's a funny story, but like most urban legends it keeps reinventing itself year after year. It's like trying to kill a snake, just when you think it's dead it comes back to life again."

Carson even discussed it on air with Fonda in 1989. When she told Carson that her son insisted it was true, he said, "No, I think I would recall that."

The story is so ingrained in people's minds that even Carson's sidekick of 30 years, Ed McMahon, seemed to recall the exchange taking place. "Let me put it this way—I can't deny that it didn't happen," McMahon told me in 2006. "I may have been off that night."

It's just the kind of quip that Carson, who died in 2005, would say and get away with, said McMahon. "Johnny was such a rascal."

McMahon also points out that TV was a much more innocent place back in the '60s and '70s. "We were always hearing from standards and practices," he said. "I don't know what happened to those standards—there seem to be no standards today and a lot more practices."

Standards and practices would have freaked if the Carson quip had happened in the '60s. In 1960, Carson's predecessor, Jack Paar, was censored for trying to tell a late night joke about a "water closet" (British slang for bathroom). A "pussy" joke in the '60s would have put NBC's very licence at risk.

Even if Carson had said it, it would never have aired. Take this actual quote from Johnny to the oft-married Zsa Zsa, circa mid-'60s: "Any girl who owns a drip-dry wedding dress can't be all bad."

Bratty, mildly risqué, maybe, but dirty? There's no way Carson would have gone there with the cat. As *TV Guide* reflected in a 1968 article, for all his reputation as an envelope pusher, "Johnny's television manners are usually as impeccable as a parson's."

Later, as standards grew more permissive in the '80s and '90s, Carson took more chances. When a female guest went on about how fans are so interested in big stars like him that they would "even just like to look at your house and your shrubs," Carson shot back, "I would love to see your shrubs."

Even Carson's famous crack to Dolly Parton in the late '70s that he would give "half a year's pay just to peek under your blouse" seems relatively tame by today's standards.

Former *Tonight Show* producer Peter Lassally—who went on to executive produce both the *Late Show with David Letterman* and *The Late Late Show with Craig Ferguson*—is certain that the Carson cat tale never took place. "Johnny said so many smart and funny things on *The Tonight Show* over the years that it's easy to assume every one of these rumors is true," Lassally said when contacted.

The question brought to mind one of Lassally's favorite Carson quips. "He was interviewing one of the *Charlie's Angels*, who wasn't quite a rocket scientist," said Lassally. "About halfway through the interview, Johnny just turned to her and said, deadpan: 'Have you ever read a book?'"

RUMOR: The wife of a famous golfer was once a guest on The Tonight Show. *Carson asked if she did anything special for her hubby before a big tournament for good luck. Her reply: "I kiss his balls." Said Carson, "That must make his putter stick out."*

FALSE: This is the one that everyone—including McMahon—swears they actually heard. As the story goes, the naughty quip got Carson suspended for several weeks.

But it never, ever happened. In the first place, why would the wife of a famous golfer (usually identified as Arnold Palmer) be a guest on *The Tonight Show*? Although he was on with Carson at least twice, Palmer confirms that his first wife Winnie (who died in 1999) never was.

The golf legend addressed the "ball" joke on *The Tonight Show* in 1994 with Carson's successor, Jay Leno, saying it was false and, besides, "I don't ever go to bed without pajamas."

This is just an example of a dirty joke attributed to a TV star known for his zingers. Variations on the "kiss his balls" joke, however, clearly predate Carson. In author Ben Alba's book, *Inventing Late Night: Steve Allen and the Original* Tonight Show, the exchange supposedly took place in the mid-'50s between golfer Sam Snead's wife, Audrey (who died in 1990), sitting in *The Tonight Show* audience, and Steve Allen.

Allen asked her, "'Does Sammy have any superstitions when he plays golf?'" writes Alba. "She answered, 'Yes, before each game I kiss his balls.'"

Allen, according to Alba, held his expression to the point of tears. The audience laughed for two solid minutes, according to frequent Allen player Steve Lawrence. "It was," he is quoted as saying, "one of the funniest deadpans that I've seen on live television."

Again, that nitwit who erased all those *Tonight Show* tapes destroyed plenty of Allen's legacy, too. The exchange, if it ever happened, cannot be checked.

Snopes.com doubts it did. It cites an even earlier reference to the "kiss his balls" joke in a July 1954 Walter Winchell column. (Allen's national NBC broadcast of *The Tonight Show* didn't premiere until September of that year, although he did host a local New York version that started in June of 1953).

The Winchell reference had the exchange between Snead's wife and John Tillman, a New York newscaster, although, as Snopes.com points out, it is hard to tell if Winchell actually witnessed the exchange, heard about it from a third party, or if it even aired.

The "kiss his balls" legend has spawned at least one parody. Uncyclopedia, which mocks the Internet information site Wikipedia, boasts a fake quote attributed to Mrs. Sam Snead, stating she saved her pucker power for Arnold Palmer. "'I used to kiss his balls to bring him luck. Sam never knew.'" As McMahon would say, "Heyyyoooo."

RUMOR: Lee Marvin appeared on The Tonight Show *in the '70s and told Carson that the bravest man he ever knew was Bob Keeshan (Captain Kangaroo) who fought beside him during one of the biggest battles of World War II.*

FALSE: According to Snopes.com, the "rumor has it" Web site, this is one that has been fueled by the Internet, circulating to millions as an inspirational and anonymous e-mail. Sometimes, the name of another famous children's entertainer, Fred Rogers, is substituted for Keeshan's. Here's the text of the Internet hoax, which was sent out to millions of individuals as dialogue purportedly taken directly from The Tonight Show:

Johnny said... "Lee, I'll bet a lot of people are unaware that you were a Marine in the initial landing at Iwo Jima...and that during the course of that action you earned the Navy Cross and were severely wounded." And you know how Lee was... "Yeah, yeah...I got shot square in the ass and they gave me the Cross for securing a hot spot about halfway up Sunbachi. Bad thing about getting shot up on a mountain is guys getting shot hauling you down.

"But Johnny, at Iwo I served under the bravest man I ever knew.... We both got the Cross that same day but what he did for his Cross made mine look cheap by comparison. The dumb bastard actually stood up on Red Beach and directed his troops to move forward to get the hell off that beach. That sergeant and I have become life-long friends.... When they brought me off Sunbachi, we passed the sergeant and he lit up a smoke and passed it to me lying on my belly in the litter... 'Where'd they get you, Lee?'... 'Well, Bob...if you make it home before me, tell Mom to sell the outhouse.'... Johnny, I'm not lying...Sgt. Keeshan was the bravest man I ever knew—Bob Keeshan...You and the world know him as Captain Kangaroo."

In my job as a newspaper TV columnist, I've had readers e-mail me about this story, demanding I write a feature to shed light on this heroic action and honor the memory of Keeshan, beloved for his 30 years as Captain Kangaroo.

Trouble is, it isn't true. Keeshan, who was in delicate health in his later years (he died at age 76 in 2004), repeatedly denied it. As he covers in his autobiography, *Good Morning Captain: 50 Wonderful Years with Bob Keeshan, TV's Captain Kangaroo*, the children's entertainer did have a military connection. He was in the U.S. Marine Corps reserves, but he was just too young and too late to see active duty during World War II, signing up just weeks before the war ended.

Marvin, however, fits the soldier legend both on- and offscreen. He seemed right at home as a jut-jawed combat veteran in *The Dirty Dozen* (1967). In real life, he had war experiences close to those described in the e-mail. Not only did he see action in World War II, but he fought at the Battle of Saipan (not Iwo Jima, which took place half a year later), was wounded in action (in the buttocks, as the e-mail suggests) and was awarded a Purple Heart (not the Navy Cross, which is an even higher honor).

He was also named after Confederate Gen. Robert E. Lee—a distant relative—and was a direct descendant of Thomas Jefferson. Can you get any more all-American?

A medical discharge from the army led to a plumber's apprentice job at a local New York theater. There he was asked to replace an ailing actor at a rehearsal which eventually led to an Oscar-winning movie career. Truth is stranger than fiction.

Marvin went on to win an Academy Award for playing two characters in the cowboy comedy *Cat Ballou* (1965). He was buried a soldier and is interred at Arlington National Cemetery. His simple tombstone makes no mention of his Oscar win, stating simply, "Lee Marvin PFC U.S. Marine Corps World War II Feb. 19, 1924 Aug. 29 1987."

The urban legend that Lee and Keeshan—two such dissimilar movie and TV stars—fought side-by-side plays to our respect and admiration for these individuals as well as the enduring power of *The Tonight Show* to drive and spread even the wildest of tall tales to a mass audience.

The other kernel of truth to this tale is that Marvin was a frequent *Tonight Show* guest, stopping by at least four times between 1970 and 1973. He might have even touched on his military service during one or two of those visits, but certainly, to Lassally's recollection, never made up the part about Bob Keeshan. And without the tapes to confirm or deny, well, tossing out all that *Tonight Show* evidence takes the full stop sign away from all these crazy rumors.

The death of Keeshan also seems to have revived this rumor. According to BreakTheChain.org, the Marvin/Keeshan e-mail only really started to pick up steam after Keeshan passed away on January 23, 2004.

There is an old saying: Don't let the truth get in the way of a great story. This is a great story. What baby boomer doesn't want to believe that one of his childhood idols was a real life war hero?

That same longing seems to have fueled a similar Internet myth: that gentle children's entertainer Fred Rogers, the cardigan-wearing host of *Mr. Rogers' Neighborhood*, was also a gun-toting war avenger. Here's the text of one of the outrageous Rogers e-mails:

> On another note, there was this wimpy little man (who just passed away) on PBS, gentle and quiet. Mr. Rogers is another one of those you would least suspect of being anything but what he now portrays to our youth. But Mr. Rogers was a U.S. Navy SEAL, combat proven in Vietnam with over 25 confirmed kills to his name. He wore a long sleeve sweater to cover the many tattoos on his forearm and biceps. A master at small arms and hand-to-hand combat, able to disarm or kill in a heartbeat, he hid that away and won our hearts with his quiet wit and charm.

Rogers, who died in 2003, was never in the military. Born in 1928, he would have been 40 when the war in Vietnam was at its terrible peak.

In 1963, when America's involvement in that war was just beginning to escalate, Rogers was ordained a Presbyterian minister. His first appearance on TV as Mister Rogers also occurred that same year, in Canada. He later returned to his hometown of Pittsburgh, where *Mister Rogers' Neighborhood* ran for 30 years on PBS.

Having met Fred Rogers on two occasions, I got the impression that he was every bit as gentle, gracious, and as peaceful as he appeared on screen. It speaks to how suspicious and cynical we have become as a society that any authority figure—even Mister Rogers—can be seen as conspiring to hide a dark, violent secret.

Thank goodness Barney or The Wiggles never appeared on *The Tonight Show*, or we might get e-mails about how they all fought together in the Gulf.

RUMOR: A Carson monologue joke about a toilet paper shortage led to a real run on bathroom tissue.

TRUE: Lassally confirms that this one did happen. Carson was doing his usual monologue on December 19, 1973, when he related a story in the news about Wisconsin congressman Harold Froehlich. Seems the politician was complaining that the U.S. government was falling behind in bids to supply the stuff.

"You know what's disappearing from the supermarket shelves? Toilet paper," Carson told his audience that night. "There's an acute shortage of toilet paper in the United States."

The next day, consumers ran to their local supermarkets and bought up as many rolls as they could carry. By noon there were empty shelves where toilet paper once stood in abundance. Sphincters tightened all across America.

Scott Paper issued statements asking the public to stay calm, and allowed the press to film their plants in full production, but panic had already set in. It took three weeks before store shelves were properly restocked.

If there was ever any doubt about the power and reach of *The Tonight Show*, the Great Toilet Paper Shortage of 1973 put those doubts to rest. Carson went back on the air a few nights later and apologized for the bum's rush. Glad we got to the bottom of it.

CHAPTER 2

Can We Talk? Other Famous Talk Show Rumors

Think talk show urban myths begin and end with *The Tonight Show*? Wrong, late night rumor breath.

Some of the strangest and most persistent rumors have attached themselves to several other talk shows, both the late night variety and the daytime talkers.

It's not so surprising given the popularity of some of these shows, especially *The Oprah Winfrey Show*, which has been a daytime staple for over 20 years and has a fevered, almost cult-like following. All Winfrey has to do is hold up a book for it to appear at the top of the bestseller list. Like, say, this book, which is colorful, lightweight, and affordable, and would make a lovely gift for a friend or eight or nine million Oprah readers.

The nature of daytime TV also lends itself to plenty of bizarre behavior. Outrageous tabloid TV shenanigans on shows hosted by Jerry Springer, Maury Povich, or Geraldo Rivera, among others, often falls into that "did I really see that?" category.

"I've always thought of the show pretty much as a cartoon," Springer told me when I interviewed him in 2006. Tune in to any episode and witness an endless parade of chair-tossing, dress-ripping, eye-gouging, dysfunctional mouth breathers.

Judge not, however, says Springer. He insists he's never met anybody who couldn't be a guest on his show. "Everyone has a story in their life that if everyone else knew..." he says, looking his accuser in the eye.

The difference, Springer says, is that "ninety percent of the world's population would never go on television and broadcast (their dysfunction)." Humiliating? That's a middle-class judgment, says Springer, the son of Holocaust survivors who came to America from England at the age of 5.

He sees his audience as regular people who want to be happy and who laugh at the jokes and get angry when they're provoked and pretty much act like everybody else. "It's an economic, cultural division rather than a moral division," says Springer, who tries to remain nonjudgmental.

His show is the real reality TV, he says, unlike fake shows like *Survivor* and *Big Brother*. "Let's take these people and put them on an island," he says. "It's not real. It's creating a false situation that you'd never really have in your life, and let's televise it."

On his show, there's no script and no net, just real people with real problems. "We had never seen that before in American television," he says.

"It's reality, but it is outrageous reality," says Springer, careful to say "outrageous" rather than "heightened."

Only nut bars need apply. Got a normal, uplifting story? Go see Oprah. "We're only allowed to take stories that are outside what is considered mainstream. If someone calls us with a warm, uplifting, positive story, we're required to send them to another show," he says.

Despite, or perhaps because of, all this outrageous behavior, there really aren't any persistent *Jerry Springer Show* rumors. It's almost as if the actual onstage antics are so over-the-top nobody would dare make any of them up. How do you top actual and typical Springer headlines such as: "My boyfriend left me for some one-armed (BLEEP)"? That was followed by a scene of two women fighting. Suddenly, a prosthetic forearm was yanked off and hurled to the floor of the Springer stage. "She'll go out on a limb to get her ex back," the narrator barks. "Hands down our best show ever."

As Springer himself declares, "This is a circus."

RUMOR: Tommy Hilfiger made racist statements about African Americans, Hispanics, and Asians on the Oprah Winfrey Show *and was asked to leave the stage.*

FALSE: Successful corporations and businesses are often the target of vicious rumors and gossip. At one time, companies existed for the sole purpose of spreading rumors. W. Howard Downey and Associates, established in 1915, were in the dirty tricks racket, specializing in rumor mongering. They actually ran ads boasting about their ability to start a hot rumor on just a few hours notice, usually by dispatching two-man teams to crowded areas and striking up conversations loaded with rumor bombs.

Most companies, hopefully, have always been above this nasty practice, but, hey, business is business. There are dozens of rumors out there, for example, linking Procter & Gamble (P&G) to satanism or Moonie cults based on no more than their mystic-looking man in the moon corporate logo (more about that later). There are even rumors that the head of McDonald's once went on a talk show and spilled the beans about how he donated gobs of money to satanic causes.

Now, in the first place, satanists prefer much spicier foods. In the second place, unless the Hamburglar is up to his old tricks again, nobody is siphoning anything off McDonald's.

Besides big companies such as P&G and McDonald's, designers like Liz Claiborne and Tommy Hilfiger have been targeted by the rumor mongers. In the case of Hilfiger, the story goes something like this:

Some time in the mid-'90s, an e-mail circulated suggesting Hilfiger supposedly gave an interview (sources range from CNN to BET to *The Ricki Lake Show* to a Philippines tabloid) where he made outrageously racist remarks. One version of the story had him joining fellow designer Ralph Lauren as a guest on *CNN Style with Elsa Klensch*. Hilfiger supposedly was quoted as saying that he was cool with his clothes being sold all around the world, but some designer duds just didn't look right on certain races. In one version of the rumor, dating back to the fall of 1996, according to Snopes.com, Hilfiger supposedly singled out Asians, saying "these people" shouldn't wear his clothing line. In another version, blacks are maligned.

A typical Hilfiger rumor e-mail contained false quotes attributed to the designer, such as, "If I'd known African Americans, Hispanics, Jewish, and Asians would buy my clothes, I would not have made them so nice. I wish these people would NOT buy my clothes, as they are made for upper class white people."

Racial rumors are a particularly nasty and persistent stain of ugliness that seem to pick up speed on the Internet. Hilfiger, whose clothes are pitched to an upscale, fashion-conscious consumer, must seem like the type of snooty blue blood who needs to be knocked down from his high horse. Or perhaps a competitor churning out cheap Hilfiger knockoffs was looking for a competitive edge at any price.

Speaking of obvious rumor mill targets, here's where Oprah comes in. The daytime talk show host supposedly had Hilfiger on her show specifically to grill him on the racist remarks and then publicly boot him off her show. The Hilfiger rumor e-mails often contained phrases like "Good for Oprah!!!!" and "BOYCOTT PLEASE...& SEND THIS MESSAGE TO ANYONE YOU KNOW."

Almost immediately, Hilfiger took measures to counter the slander. In a statement first posted on his Web site in 1997 and still there a decade later (under the heading "Rumor" in the "Company Information" area), it states that he "did not make the alleged inappropriate racial comments." It goes on to say that Hilfiger "wants his clothing to be enjoyed by people of all backgrounds" and that he features "models of all ethnic backgrounds" in all his advertising.

Hilfiger himself is quoted, saying, "I am deeply unhappy and frustrated that a malicious and completely erroneous rumor continues to circulate about me on the Internet." Anti-Defamation League (ADL) national director Abraham H. Foxman also came to Hilfiger's defense, stating that the ADL had run their own investigation and concluded that "the malicious rumors circulating about you and your company are without merit and lack any basis in fact."

Several denials have also appeared over the years in mainstream media. In a 1997 article in the *Los Angeles Times* ("When Rumors Are Clothed in Truth"), it was reported that Hilfiger had never appeared as a guest on either *CNN Style with Elsa Klensch* or *Oprah Winfrey*. An article in the *Buffalo News* early in 1999 restated the denials, with *Oprah Winfrey* spokesperson Audrey Pass stating that Hilfiger had never been a guest on the show.

The rumor was so persistent and far-reaching that Winfrey herself finally had to address it on the air. On Monday, January 11, 1999, she began her show by saying that she wanted to "set the record straight once and for all."

> The rumor claims that clothing designer Tommy Hilfiger came on the show and made racist remarks, and that I then kicked him out. I just want to say that this is not true because it just never happened. Tommy Hilfiger has never appeared on this show. Read my lips, Tommy Hilfiger has never appeared on this show.

Winfrey went on to state that she had never even met the designer.

Did the rumor affect sales? According to a U.S. Tommy Hilfiger spokesperson, Catherine Fisher, who spoke with *TV Guide* in 1999, it did not. She also noted at the time that the rumor had already begun to show signs of diminishing.

RUMOR: *Joan Rivers once blurted out Victoria Principal's home phone number on national TV.*

TRUE: Can we talk? Rivers sure can, and in 1986 she blurted out something that ended up costing big money.

The tart-tongued comedian had been a comedy veteran for years when she was named the first-ever permanent guest host of *The Tonight Show Starring Johnny Carson* in 1983. Rivers sparkled in her guest star role, spiking *The Tonight Show*'s ratings, especially among younger viewers. A little of Joan, it was concluded, went a long way.

The then fledgling FOX network saw an opportunity to get into the lucrative late night TV market. They lured Rivers away from NBC and *The Tonight Show* and gave Rivers her own show opposite Carson in the fall of 1986.

This infuriated Carson, who found out about the defection from his producer. He saw Rivers's move as an enormous betrayal and never spoke to her again. Rivers tried to joke about the rift at the time ("I'm the only woman who ever left him and didn't ask for money," she joked), but the defection led to booking wars and other late night nastiness.

So the stakes were high and personal when *The Late Show Starring Joan Rivers* premiered in October 1986. At first, Rivers was a big success, but, as the weeks wore on, the novelty of Rivers five nights a week wore off and viewers switched back to Carson. After seven months, Rivers was out of late night.

Into the middle of this scrap waded Victoria Principal. The sexy *Dallas* star became a favorite Rivers target, especially after she married a plastic surgeon. "Isn't that convenient...and free," taunted Rivers in a typical monologue jab.

The feud dated back to Rivers's days on *The Tonight Show*. Principal had been a guest on that show in 1983. Rivers, as she recalled in her 1991 autobiography, *Still Talking*, caught Principal in a lie. The host wanted to gossip about Principal's breakup with Andy Gibb, younger brother of the Bee Gees clan. Gibb and Principal had once been engaged. "Did you keep the ring?" Rivers asked. Principal denied there was ever any ring or engagement. "But you showed me one," Rivers told her startled guest. "You and Andy Gibb came to my dressing room in Las Vegas. You had the ring, you had just gotten engaged."

Principal, naturally, was miffed. "I'll get you next time," she told the talk show host after the show. There was another *Tonight Show* visit, and this time Rivers caught Principal lying about her age. The actress claimed she was born in 1950, the first American baby born in Japan after the war.

Rivers pointed out that the war ended five years earlier, in 1945. Maybe they were both born in 1950, Rivers cracked. "Where did you buy your birth certificate?" Principal asked. "Same place you bought yours," Rivers hissed.

Principal apparently stormed off after the show. Rivers, however, wasn't through. Later that season, she had Gibb as a guest and he confirmed the engagement and the ring. Rivers asked Gibb how old Principal was when the couple broke up two years earlier. "Same age she is now, I think," he joked.

So the feud was still raging when Rivers had one of Principal's *Dallas* costars, Ken Kercheval, on as a guest on her own late night talk show in December of 1986. Rivers used Kercheval's presence as an excuse to phone Principal, live, on the air. The actress's birthday was coming up, and Rivers saw another chance to stick in the needle.

At first, all Rivers got were busy signals. The nervy host then asked the operator to break into the line, claiming the call was an emergency. In order to do that, Rivers had to repeat Principal's private, unlisted home phone number over the air.

Whoops. A few weeks later, reports surfaced that Principal had filed a suit against the comedienne, seeking $3 million in damages. She claimed she was flooded with phone calls and that her privacy had been invaded. "We think (Rivers's) conduct was malicious, provocative, beyond the bounds of decency, and a violation of Victoria's right to privacy," said her attorney at the time, who couldn't resist adding, "I guess we'll see how funny she is in a court of law."

The suit was apparently settled out of court. For how much? For once, the "Can we talk?" comedienne wasn't talking, but Principal did hint to *TV Guide* in a 1993 article that it was a substantial sum. "Come and see my Picasso," she cooed.

RUMOR: *An executive from P&G once went on* Sally Jesse Raphael *(or Phil Donahue, Merv Griffin, Oprah Winfrey, or Maury Povich) and admitted that he was a devil worshiper.*

FALSE: *It's usually a tip-off that the rumor is a hoax when it is attributed to a variety of possible sources. Other versions of this rumor have this anonymous executive spilling the beans about his company and devil worship on 20/20 or 60 Minutes. The story usually includes the line that the corporation donates 10 percent of its earning to satanic organizations.*

And that's where this devil of a rumor really falls apart. Imagine a corporation giving away a percentage of its earnings. Ridiculous!

This rumor appears to date back to around 1980, when news reports escalated about the Reverend Sun Myung Moon and his Unification Church (since renamed the Family Federation for World Peace and Unification). Mass weddings among Moon followers (dubbed "Moonies") made worldwide headlines.

Around the same time, somebody took a second look at P&G's old-fashioned, mystical-looking logo—a circle with a crescent-shaped, bearded man in the moon gazing at 13 stars—and concluded that P&G was a front for the Moonies.

If you connect the dots from the moon man's curly beard to the 13 stars, so the story goes, you will get 3 sixes (or, just to add another crazy level to all of this, the mirror image of 3 sixes), which, as everyone who watches horror movies knows, is the sign of the beast. (I used to work at the *Toronto Sun*, whose offices were located at 333 King Street, prompting one interview subject to comment that the place must be only half satanic.)

The truth is that the P&G logo is one of the oldest corporate symbols in American business. The trademark dates back to the 1850s, when P&G was primarily a candle and soap maker. Wooden crates of their products were stamped or marked with a simple star in a circle, a reference to the Cincinnati, Ohio–based company's "star" brand candles. Later, the company founders (William Procter, a candlemaker, and James Gamble, a soap manufacturer) worked 13 stars into the logo, a patriotic salute to America's founding 13 colonies. By the 1860s, the moon and stars logo could be found on all P&G products, as well as the company's stationery.

When the Moonie rumors first surfaced around 1980, a spokesperson for P&G immediately denied any connection. The premise, it was pointed out, was absurd. The world's biggest consumer goods company, with products like Tide, Crest, Ivory, and Pampers in households throughout the world, P&G is publicly traded and profits are carefully audited and shared with stockholders, not cult members.

Still, the rumor spread, eventually linking the consumer giant with satanism instead of the Moonies. By the middle of 1982, calls to a P&G toll-free hotline about the rumor were averaging 600 a day. A 1991 report suggested that the company had fielded more than 150,000 letters and phone calls up to that point about the false cult connection.

What drove this rumor? What else, but the rumor box. Most of the friend of a friends who heard about it claimed it was verified on television.

Snopes.com dates one version to 1994, with *The Phil Donahue Show* named as the source. The talk show host supposedly asked the P&G executive if coming out in support of Satan wasn't a bad business move. To which the executive replied (and here's where the "cyber myth" switches to all caps), "THERE ARE NOT ENOUGH CHRISTIANS IN THE UNITED STATES TO MAKE A DIFFERENCE."

Now, three-quarters of all Americans practice or follow a Christian faith. Clearly, somebody was hoping the millions of American Christians would stand up and say, "Oh yeah?" and boycott the toothpaste and toiletries giant.

This naturally alarmed executives at the company, who were anxious to prove they were, like their soap, still 99.44/100 percent pure. P&G and their lawyers zeroed in on individuals at Amway Corporation, for spreading the rumor with malicious intent. One of P&G's direct competitors, Amway, now known as Alticor, is a door-to-door consumer goods company. One Amway distributor was alleged to have left a version of the TV show rumor on the company's voice mail system, where it was picked up and spread by other distributors.

In March of 2007, a Salt Lake City court awarded a $19.25 million settlement to P&G in a suit brought against four former Amway distributors. "This is about protecting out reputation," P&G legal officer Jim Johnson said in a statement. The company has spent millions suing anyone they thought might have spread this malicious rumor, and they have had other successes in court.

In the '80s, the company also appealed to religious leaders, including Billy Graham and Jerry Falwell, to help spread the word to their congregations that P&G still stood for pure and good. They also took out ads debunking the rumors and explaining the true origins of their unusual logo.

As usual, there is a whiff of credibility to the TV aspect of this rumor, which probably helped make it stick. Donahue, a popular, white-haired talk show host, often featured consumer advocates such as Ralph Nader on his television program. A mix of tabloid and topical, his show ran nationally for 27 years (plus two seasons as a local show out of Dayton, Ohio) before going off the air in 1996.

Throughout that long run, however, according to a spokesperson, the show never, ever featured an executive from P&G.

Still, the rumor would just not go away. A later version of the rumor had the unnamed P&G executive blurting the cult connection on *Sally Jesse Raphael*, supposedly on March 1, 1998. (Which, as it turns out, was a Sunday, a day of rest, even for Raphael.)

Raphael, whose show went off the air in 2002 after a 19-year run, eventually posted a disclaimer on the "frequently asked question" section of her Web site. "The president of Procter and Gamble has NEVER appeared on

The Sally Show...NEVER," it read. "Nor has any other person in authority at P&G." The disclaimer went on to say that if somebody had blurted such an outrageous claim, "We would have scored a broadcasting scoop and would have trumpeted it to all the newspapers."

In other words, don't believe everything you don't read in the papers.

The fallout from all of this is that P&G yanked their man-in-the-moon logo off all their products in the mid-'80s when it was clear that this malicious rumor was having a direct impact on sales of their products. In 1985—the same year the logo began to disappear—P&G suffered its first decline in earnings since 1953.

In 1991, the old moon man was replaced with a simple new "P&G" letter logo. A spokesperson for Satan says he is looking for a new corporation to bedevil.

RUMOR: R&B singer Ciara revealed to Oprah Winfrey that she was once a man.

FALSE: The things people tell Oprah. Everybody comes prepared to open up, girlfriend. At least that's the impression that helps drive wild rumors like this one.

Ciara Princess Harris was born on October 25, 1985, in Austin, Texas. There is not the slightest bit of evidence that the Grammy Award winner was ever a prince.

While still a teenager and barely out of high school, the pop and hip-hop singer—now down to one name, Ciara—had a hit album (*Goodies*) and several dance singles on the charts.

Early in 2005, an Internet rumor began to circulate that Ciara had been born a hermaphrodite or "intersexual." Word was Ciara spilled the beans on *The Oprah Winfrey Show*. She supposedly blabbed to the talk show host about getting a sex change operation at the tender age of five.

Ciara herself has heard and denied this rumor. She was quoted in the *New York Daily News* saying that the rumor was funny. "I've never been on *Oprah* in my life," she declared.

Here is what happened. A transsexual in Ireland, also named Ciara, has a Web site where he goes into detail about his surgical gender switch. The Irish-born Ciara, about 20 years older, was born male and went under the knife in 1999.

Clearly, some Ciara music fans Googled the singer and got their Irish up. The she that used to be a he was mistaken for the she that's still a she. Got it?

Remember, Ciara's first album was called *Goodies*. Ba-dump-dump.

The good news for Oprah is that hers is seen as the show where the stars will tell all. Tom Cruise's couch-hopping histrionics probably set the bar a little higher. If Tom-Tom can become all unglued over Katie Holmes on Oprah, well, anything can happen.

RUMOR: The Young & The Restless's *Eileen Davidson told TV's Phil Donahue that she was born a man.*

FALSE: He/she whodunits turned up years before Ciara was even born. In the mid-'80s, a rumor started to circulate that Eileen Davidson, who played Ashley Abbott for several years on The Young and the Restless (Y&R), *was originally a man.*

No wonder some wise guys called the show *The Hung and the Breastless.*

This rumor stuck for decades despite Davidson, who also appeared on *Days of Our Lives* and *Santa Barbara*, being voted one of the most beautiful women in daytime drama by *Soap Opera Digest.*

Davidson herself addressed the rumor in a 1999 *TV Guide* article (the same year she returned to Y&R). "People swear they saw me on *Donahue* talking about my surgery," she said.

Davidson feels she was confused with Caroline Cossey, a transgender model who works under the name Tula, who has similar, angular features. Tula was born in England as Barry Kenneth Cossey and became the first transgendered model to appear nude in *Playboy.* She also had a small part in the James Bond movie *For Your Eyes Only,* thus becoming the first Bond Girl who wasn't born a girl. Talk about shaken, not stirred.

As the Snopes.com site points out, however, Tula did not appear on *Donahue* until June 29, 1990—three years after a newspaper article mentioned the "Davidson is a man" rumor and about five years after the rumor first surfaced.

The rumor may have been stirred in 1998. During that season, Davidson appeared as quadruplets on *Days Of Our Lives*—one of them being a man.

Still, Davidson is pretty sure she's a she. "I never appeared on *Donahue* and I am not a transsexual," she declared. Being the target of a wild rumor has made her very cynical about any Hollywood reports she reads. "I don't believe any rumors because it could be as full of bullshit as this one," she told *TV Guide*'s long time soap columnist Michael Logan.

As for trying to dispel the gossip, "Why bother?" says Davidson. "I could stand naked in Yankee Stadium and they'd say, 'She had a great surgeon,'" she told Logan. "I could remind people I'm married and they'd say, 'Oh, puh-leez, out there in Hollywood, anything goes!'"

Davidson has, in fact, been married three times. She and third hubby Vince Van Patten welcomed a son, Jesse, in 2003. Hopefully he hasn't heard the rumor—yet.

RUMOR: A psychic on a popular talk show predicted that a mass murder would take place on a college campus that Halloween.

FALSE: Here's your classic spooky story told around the electronic hearth. Over the years, psychics and mentalists have made appearances on the Late Show with David Letterman, The Tonight Show, *or, farther back,* The Mike Douglas Show, *and have performed astounding stunts. They've correctly identified cards and numbers that were apparently chosen at random. Some, like the Amazing Kreskin, have even predicted election outcomes.*

A much more morbid legend has made the rounds for years, dating back all the way to the '60s. In this one, a psychic went on a talk show (everything from *Donahue* to *Geraldo* to *Tonight Show Starring Johnny Carson* to *Oprah* has been cited) and predicts a terrible mass murder will take place. Some hatchet-wielding maniac (sometimes described as dressed like Little Bo Peep) is about to hack down as many as 20 students at a university campus, the seer warns. After which, Carson, or Montel Williams, or Winfrey, or whoever, presumably cut to a commercial for Gillette blades or Bounty paper towels, "The quicker picker upper."

The grim fable seems spun straight out of any of a dozen slasher films where students are terrorized by various hockey mask-wearing Jasons or Freddy Kruegers. That it predates those films suggests it was inspired by real life murders, such as the slaying of nine nurses by Richard Speck in Chicago in the mid-'60s.

Articles about various mass murder rumors have appeared in dozens of college campus newspapers over the years, no doubt keeping more than a few dorm lights on at night. The target was often a Big Ten school and the predicted date was usually Halloween night.

In a 1998 article titled, "Urban Legend Strikes U," the *Michigan State News* suggested that "Students need not fear a Halloween massacre this year." In this version, Michigan State University (MSU) are the supposed targets. The murders were supposed to take place in H-shaped dorms or halls that began with the letter H. Another clue to the whereabouts was that a railway track would be close to the targeted murder site. It was all apparently outlined in detail on—where else—*The Oprah Winfrey Show.*

"I'm scared," a freaked out freshman who lives in Michigan State's Holden Hall, an H-shaped dorm near a railway track, is quoted as saying. "I'm going to the fraternity house for the weekend. I don't care if it is true or not. I'm not waiting around to find out."

Not helping when this story was published was the recent release of *Urban Legend,* a film that featured a similar campus murder tale. The film was cashing in on the whole Halloween horror film craze, and if a few rumors could drum up some extra publicity (as well as inspire several stories on college newspapers), so much the better.

Oprah spokesperson Audrey Pass was once again summoned to dismiss the grisly gossip. "We never had such a show. There was never such a thing said," said Pass.

RUMOR: David Letterman once read a Top Ten List which made fun of why there were no black NASCAR drivers.

FALSE: Sadly, there are dozens and dozens of racially motivated myths and legends. Most are just racist attacks disguised as jokes. Retelling them just perpetuates them.

Still, it is the dark side of the culture of the urban myth and should be dissected and understood. Racism travels and has for centuries.

While Letterman has taken shots at just about everything and everyone over the years, that he would make fun of such a sensitive topic is unthinkable. Two things he loves are racing (he is part owner of Team Rahal) and fellow comedians. One of his first jobs in show business was writing jokes for Jimmy "J. J." Walker. Many other black comedians, including Bill Cosby, George Wallace, and Bernie Mac, have been warmly embraced on his show. So make fun of racers? Absolutely. Make fun of race? Never.

The other giveaway about the phony Top Ten list, which circulated on the Internet in 2005, is (a) it is overtly rednecked and (b) it is not very funny. (For example, number seven, "Pit crew can't work on car while holding up their pants at the same time," and number three, "No Cadillacs approved for competition").

Other jokes made fun of rap music, "hos," and pistols under the front seat.

Letterman has had real race car drivers on to read Top Ten Lists. In 1999, Dale Jarrett read "Top Ten NASCAR Driver Pet Peeves" which featured the following: number eight, "Kids in the back keep asking, 'Are we at lap 236 yet?'" and number six, "You're doing 200, and Letterman still passes you."

See, now that is funny.

CHAPTER 3

Ward, I'm Worried about the Beaver: TV Rumors Involving Child Stars

The death of a former teen or child star is one of TV's most persistent rumors. Besides *Leave It to Beaver* tyke Jerry Mathers, it has dogged Adam Rich from *Eight Is Enough*, *Saved by the Bell*'s Mark-Paul Gosselaar, *Full House*'s Jodie Sweetin, and even little Mikey of Life cereal fame, who supposedly died from the explosive effects of mixing Pop Rocks candy with soda. (See the chapter on commercial rumors.)

One of the earliest examples centers around the original *Mickey Mouse Club*. That daily children's series was such a sensation when it premiered in the mid-1950s that the young unknown "Mouseketeers" became instant celebrities. According to Lorranie Santoli, author of *The Official Mickey Mouse Club Book* (Hyperion, 1995), it wasn't long before ghoulish rumors spread that Cubby O'Brien or Annette Funicello or one of the other popular cast members had been killed in a car accident or some other mishap. The rumors became so persistent that the Disney studio issued a press release in 1956 titled "Mouseketeers Alive and Squeaking," assuring fans that everybody was not just "neat and pretty" but also alive and well.

The Mouseketeers, it could be argued, were TV's first American idols, ordinary kids turned into instant pop stars through television. To young viewers at the time, they were as familiar as kids at school. Seeing them five days a week and then not seeing them for a summer may have been traumatic enough for death rumors to spread even while the series was still on the air.

More typical are child star rumors that spread years after a series has been canceled. This also allows time for child stars to grow up and run head first into adult reality. The fact that a couple of young actors really did meet early and tragic ends (including *Make Room for Daddy*'s Rusty Hamer and *Family Affair* moppet Anissa Jones) has given all child stars a black eye. For every Ron Howard (beloved as Opie on *The Andy Griffith Show* and now one of Hollywood's top directors), there seem to be dozens of Danny Bonaduces (lippy redhead Danny from *The Partridge Family* who detailed his drug addiction and other transgressions in his tell-all autobiography, *Random Acts of Badness*). "There's nothing wrong with getting rich and famous," says Paul Petersen, who starred for eight seasons in the 1950s and '60s as rambunctious teen Jeff Stone on *The Donna Reed Show*. "The trouble starts when that starts to slip away."

Petersen is founder of A Minor Consideration (www.minorcon.org), which advocates on behalf of hundreds of current and former child stars. When I spoke with him in 1998 at one of the Hollywood Collectors and Celebrities Shows in Los Angeles, Petersen joked that the group deals with everything "from heroin to hangnails."

Petersen, who was also briefly a Mouseketeer, had to overcome his own struggles with alcohol and depression. He formed the group after three former child actors all committed suicide within a few months of each other in 1989/90: Tim Hovey, who appeared on everything from *Lassie* to *Playhouse 90* in the '50s; Trent Lehman, who acted on *Nanny and the Professor* in the early '70s and who hanged himself at the age of 20; and Hamer, who spent 14 seasons on *The Danny Thomas Show*.

Fate can be cruel; Hovey, who died of a drug overdose at 44, appears next to Ron and Clint Howard—together with Jodie Foster, the shining examples of young actors gone right—in most child star directories.

Hamer was by far the most famous of the three. He was just six when he began playing Thomas's wisecracking son Rusty Williams. Fellow cast members (and audiences) were amazed at how he stepped up like a seasoned second banana, trading quips with Thomas like a Borscht Belt veteran.

He was also just six when his father died and he became his family's main source of income. Out of work and washed up at 20, Hamer drifted into a series of odd jobs. Depressed and delusional at 42, he died of a self-inflicted gunshot wound, pointing a .357 Magnum at his head and pulling the trigger.

Petersen is quick to point out that there have been relatively few former child star deaths since A Minor Consideration was formed in 1991. (River Phoenix, who died of a massive drug overdose in 1993, was one he singled out.) Still, as long as ex-Mousketeers like Britney Spears forget to put on their panties or ding dongs like *Saved by the Bell*'s Dustin Diamond continue to bust ex-Sweathogs on celebrity boxing specials or appear in their own amateur porn films, ex-child stars will continue to have a bad name.

As the 2003 David Spade comedy *Dickie Roberts: Former Child Star* (tagline: "50 million people used to watch him on TV. Now he washes their cars.") suggests, people seem predisposed to the notion that child actors are generally scarred for life and that most come to a bad end. That's generally all you need for a rumor to take root.

RUMOR: Jerry Mathers, the young actor who played adorable Beaver Cleaver for six seasons on Leave It to Beaver *(1957–63), grew up to become a soldier and was killed in Vietnam.*

FALSE: This one roared through every schoolyard and living room back in the late '60s. The idea that this all-American kid was killed in that increasingly unwinnable war must have made perfect sense to an American public growing more disheartened and disillusioned by the month.

The truth is that Mathers, who was born in 1948, never went to Vietnam. Like another all-American icon—President George W. Bush—he served in the Air Force National Guard during that war.

With the antiwar movement in full churn, the army was not going to risk having a beloved ex-child star's name in the almost daily list of Vietnam casualties. Ironically, even though they kept him out of the war, that's what happened anyway.

In many ways, the Cleavers of *Leave It to Beaver* embodied the ideal all-American family at mid-century. Dad, Ward (Hugh Beaumont), was stern and authoritarian, the undisputed head of the household. Mom, June (Barbara Billingsley), was the perfect stay-at-home housekeeper, every curl and pearl in place as she cooked, cleaned, and sewed.

The series, which ran on two networks over six seasons, told gentle little parables about growing up in America. Every week, Beav would get into some gosh darn kind of a mess and every week he'd get out of it again, all in less than half an hour.

Since America had grown up with this TV tyke, the idea that he had been killed in Vietnam hit home like a death in the family.

The rumor can be traced back to June 4, 1967, when Mathers, who turned 19 two days earlier, was seen on TV presenting the Outstanding Children's Program Emmy award to *Jack and the Beanstalk* producer and Hollywood legend Gene Kelly. What made Mathers's appearance memorable at the time, besides the fact that he hadn't been seen on TV since *Beaver* went off the air in 1963, was that he was dressed in his brand new Air Force National Guard uniform.

About a year later, the bureau chiefs of the Associated Press and United Press International were scanning casualty lists from the Vietnam War for their wire service reports. According to Mathers, who has addressed this rumor for years, that's when another Mathers—or someone with a similar name—was listed as killed in action in Vietnam.

A search through databases containing records of U.S. military officers and soldiers who died as a result of military action during the Vietnam War turned up one Steven Allen Mathers, an army sergeant, who died on October 26, 1968, and a Jerome "Jerry" Mathews, a private who was killed in action on July 12, 1968.

"Someone saw the same name or a similar name, pulled my obituary file, and ran it," Mathers recounted in an 1998 AOL Internet chat, as well as in his autobiography, . . . *And Jerry Mathers as the Beaver*, released that same year.

Keep in mind that this was shortly after the shocking assassinations of both Martin Luther King, Jr., and Robert Kennedy. America had never been more freaked.

According to Mathers, actress Shelley Winters read the report, went on *The Tonight Show Starring Johnny Carson*, and blurted the sad (and erroneous) news to millions.

Uh oh. *The Tonight Show*, circa the late '60s. This is like rocket fuel for urban legends.

The problem is that the vast majority of the tapes from the first 10 years of *The Tonight Show Starring Johnny Carson*—all the years the late night talk show originated from New York, from 1962 to 1972—are gone. As mentioned in chapter one, they aren't missing, they aren't stolen, they were erased. NBC thought reusing the tapes would be a good way to save money. As Carson would say, "Wrong, eraser breath." So no tape exists of Shelley Winters talking to Carson about Jerry Mathers being killed in Vietnam.

Two-time Oscar-winner Winters is also gone, having passed away in early 2006 at 85. She was a frequent *Tonight Show* guest, however (the Internet Movie Database (IMDb) clocks her at 21 guest appearances between 1970 and 1991), and supposedly made the remark about Mathers on the December 22, 1969, broadcast.

Winters was even asked about the famous Beaver tale in a 1998 *TV Guide* article. "I've always felt terrible about saying that," she told the magazine.

When contacted about the urban legend, Mathers's TV brother, Tony Dow (who played Beav's older brother Wally), just shook his head. Dow seemed to recall that, upon hearing the news, his family sent flowers and a letter of condolence to Mathers's family.

Over the years, he's heard 'em all, including that Ken Osmond, who played Wally's creepy pal, Eddie Haskell, grew up to become Alice Cooper. Another was that Osmond had a second career as the notoriously endowed porn star John Holmes (see the chapter on mistaken identities).

Fortunately for Mathers, he never had to deal with any urban legends about having grown up to become a porn star. He was still the Beaver—although he was now playing a divorced dad—when he returned to TV in the mid-'80s in *Still the Beaver*. Several other members of the original *Leave it to Beaver* cast, including Billingsley, Dow, and Osmond, also appeared on that mercifully short-lived cable series.

Mathers still takes the occasional acting gig. He even made a cameo in the 2006 movie *Larry the Cable Guy: Health Inspector*. Unfortunately no one saw that movie (Jay Leno called it, "Larry the Straight to Cable Guy")—and the Mathers rumor lives on.

RUMOR: Lauren Chapin, the tyke who played youngest daughter Kitten on the '50s family sitcom Father Knows Best, *later turned to prostitution.*

TRUE: Kitten a sordid sex kitten? Sad but true, although there is a happy ending.

Chapin was just eight years old when she began portraying Kathy "Kitten" Anderson on the popular black and white sitcom *Father Knows Best* (1953–60). Future *Marcus Welby* star Robert Young played her all-knowing dad and movie star Jane Wyatt her always-there mom. Billy Gray and Elinor Donahue played her teen siblings Bud and Betty.

The series presented a glossy, paternalistic, some would say too perfect, picture of family life in America at mid century. Years later, Gray denounced the show, saying "the dialogue, the situations, the characters—they were all totally false." He hated that the girls on the series "were always trained to use their feminine wiles, to pretend to be helpless to attract men." Basically, while he felt the show was "well motivated," he also felt it was a "hoax."

That probably sounds harsh to people who grew up with the Anderson family. More harsh was what happened to Chapin in real life after the series ended. (Especially since it didn't have to end. The series achieved its highest ratings the year it ceased production. Young decided he had had enough and wanted to go out on top, which hardly ever happens in television.)

Chapin's own upbringing was nothing like the supportive family life her character enjoyed. It was, in fact, a living nightmare. Among the many sad details in her moving 1989 memoir, *Father Does Know Best: The Lauren Chapin*

Story, her father, William, sexually molested her, as did her father's friend. Her mother, Marguerite, was an abusive alcoholic. Her brother beat her. Her first suicide attempt came when she was just 10 years old.

Chapin was 14 when *Father Knows Best* went off the air. Out of work and no longer the adorable tyke, her teenage years were even more traumatic and depressing. At just 16, she married auto mechanic Gerald Jones. The next year, she suffered the first of eight miscarriages. By 18, she was divorced and with an abusive boyfriend she described as "the devil incarnate." He got her hooked on heroin and pushed her into prostitution. The sick sell, reasoned the boyfriend/pimp, was that men would pay extra to have sex with Kitten.

Chapin later confessed on *The Oprah Winfrey Show* that she could never live up to the wholesome expectations of her TV character. Everyone told her she was the "best, the brightest, and the cutest." Nobody wanted to know the real Lauren, she told the talk show host, "they just wanted to know Kitten."

For the next several years, Chapin was in and out of prisons and mental institutions. There were more acid trips and self-destructive acts, including one attempt to chop off her hand with a meat cleaver. That she didn't wind up dead like too many ex-child stars is a miracle.

The birth of her son Matthew in 1973 got her started on a recovery, but it was a religious conversion in 1979, she says, that really turned her life around.

Chapin went on to be a founding member of A Minor Consideration, a group that advocates on behalf of child stars. She's also managed young singers and actors, including Jennifer Love Hewitt, played *Father Knows Best* mom Margaret Anderson on cruise line versions of the series, and was named honorary mayor of cities in Oklahoma, Texas, and Florida.

In recent years, through charity work and public appearances, the ordained evangelical minister has also helped to raise over two million dollars for underprivileged and abused children. It has been a long, rocky road, but the mother of two seems to have finally found peace and contentment in her 60s.

RUMOR: Adam Rich, who played adorable tyke Nicholas on the '70s drama Eight Is Enough, *was murdered in the '90s by a desperate, out-of-work Los Angeles stagehand.*

FALSE: Here's an example of irony gone all out of control—an ex-child star agreeing to create and spread his own urban legend about his death.

Not only is this one false, but it was fabricated on purpose—and with Rich's full cooperation—by *Might* magazine, a small San Francisco-based bimonthly.

Born in 1968, the helmet-haired moppet is best remembered from his five seasons as Nicholas Bradford on *Eight Is Enough*. He also appeared opposite Lorne Greene in the short-lived drama *Code Red* and worked everything from *The Love Boat* to *Silver Spoons* in the '70s and '80s.

After *Eight Is Enough*, Rich became another poster boy for bad ex-child star behavior, getting nabbed for substance abuse and pleading no contest to felony burglary and drug-related charges in 1992.

How sad is it when you are bailed out of jail, not by a real parent, but by your TV dad? That's exactly what happened to Rich when *Eight Is Enough* patriarch Dick Van Patten sprung his former TV teen after a 1991 pharmacy breaking and entering bust.

By 2003, he had checked himself into rehab at the Betty Ford Center. At the end of David Spade's *Dickie Roberts: Former Child Star*, released that same year, Rich (part of an "all-star" chorus of former child actors) gamely sings, "Eight rehabs isn't enough, but I've done and seen the most killer stuff."

Several years earlier, in 1996, *Might* magazine, a satiric and short-lived little bimonthly published by Dave Eggers (as he chronicles in his book, *A Heartbreaking Work of Staggering Genius*), concocted a hoax with Rich as the star player. The article suggested Rich had been murdered in a robbery-related attack by an "unemployed dinner theater stagehand" named Tad Michael Earnhardt.

In an article that appeared in *Salon* (titled, "He's Hot, He's Sexy, but He Isn't Dead"), Eggers outlined his hoax. He explained that he needed an ex-child star "famous enough to have wide name recognition, but had to have been out of the spotlight long enough that readers wouldn't question too closely why they hadn't heard about the demise."

Rich, at a career dead end at 30, was contacted and quickly agreed to play along with the gag. He sent photos from his cutesy *Eight Is Enough* days and posed for new shots to go with the article. The cover line read, "Adam Rich, 1968–1996; Fare Thee Well, Gentle Friend. His Final Days. His Last Interview. The Legacy He Leaves."

The tabloid TV magazine *Hard Copy* almost fell for the gag, writes Eggers. *Might*'s cover was blown, however, when the *National Enquirer* called Rich's publicist and got Rich himself to confirm that he was still alive. Rich then was flooded with calls from radio stations, relatives, and former girlfriends all wanting to know why they weren't invited to the funeral. Because I'm not dead, Rich tried to explain.

He later faxed out a press statement insisting he was still alive and declaring, "Personally, I believe that if you can't laugh at yourself, you've missed the biggest goddamn joke in your life. Thanks for caring, and lighten the fuck up."

There have been several other celebrity death hoaxes over the years. One involved former *Saturday Night Live* funnyman Will Ferrell, who reportedly died in a paragliding accident in March of 2006. Ferrell was reported as 36 (wrong, he was 38 at the time), a graduate of the University of California (wrong, Southern California), and dead (also wrong).

The *Bewitched* and *Elf* star had nothing to do with the report, which was posted by an untraceable source on the iNewswire Web site. Ferrell's publicist was quick to shoot down the rumor. He pointed out that his client wasn't dead, just shooting a movie in Canada. Some in Hollywood regard that as good as dead.

RUMOR: Susan Olsen, who played Cindy Brady on TV's The Brady Bunch, *committed suicide.*

FALSE: This one simply seems to be a case of mistaken identity. Olsen, the "youngest one in curls" from the popular '60s sitcom, is frequently confused with Anissa Jones, another dimpled TV moppet who played youngest child Buffy on the '60s' sitcom Family Affair. *That series starred Brian Keith as swingin' Manhattan bachelor Bill Davis. When Davis's brother and sister-in-law die in an accident, he agrees to take in the three orphaned children— young twins Buffy (Jones) and Jody (Johnny Whitaker) and their teenage sister Cissy (Kathy Garver). Taking care of them all was bearded gentleman butler Mr. French (Sebastian Cabot).*

Cute little Jones stood out with her floppy blonde pigtails and her ever-present doll, Mrs. Beasley. By June of 1969, the sitcom was a number one hit. A Mattel spin-off Beasley doll became the top-selling doll in America. Buffy paper dolls, a line of children's clothes, and even a Buffy cookbook followed.

Reports of Jones's death in August of 1976 came as a total shock to fans who remembered her as this sweet little girl on TV. Listed as the first TV star to die of a drug overdose on the Former Child Star Central Web site, the petite Indiana-native (just four foot eleven) was found to have ingested a lethal combination of cocaine, angel dust, Quaaludes, and Seconal. The San Diego County coroner said it was one of the most severe drug overdose cases that he had ever seen.

It was a shock to her old costars as well. "I had no idea she had slipped so far," Whittaker told me in 1998. At the time, he had been out of acting about five years, but his agent had run into Jones in more recent years and had seen a decline in her mood and manner.

Jones's sad real life family affair must have contributed to her troubles; her story is heartbreaking. Her parents went through a bitter divorce in 1965—the year before *Family Affair* premiered—with Anissa and her younger brother Paul, who often accompanied her to the set of *Family Affair*, caught in a petty tug-of-war custody battle. In 1973, after the series ended, custody was awarded to her father, John P. Jones. Soon after, however, he died of heart disease. Anissa rebelled against her mother, dropped out of school, and often lived with friends. She was classified a runaway and spent time in juvenile hall. There was no Mr. French to the rescue, although TV dad Keith did reportedly offer her work on his next series, *The Brian Keith Show*, which she turned down.

When she turned 18, Jones, who had briefly worked at a donut shop, came into the money she earned from the series. Approximately $180,000 had been invested in U.S. savings bonds and other trust funds. According to the Web site Morbidly Hollywood, Jones splurged on a new Ford Pinto for herself and a fully loaded Camaro for her brother. They rented an apartment together and embarked on night after night of unchecked partying; six months later, she was dead.

On August 28, 1976, after one last drug binge, she was found in the bedroom of a friend's house, dead in her sleep. Eight years after that, her brother Paul also died of a drug overdose. Jones has inspired no less than three songs about her short life and death. In 1977, the Toronto-based punk band The Diodes released a song called "Child Star." One of the unsettling lyrics went, "Uncle Bill/Uncle Bill/I took some pills/Mr. French/Mr. French/ I'm feeling tense." Other references to Jones can be heard in "Rerun Heaven" (1980) by Nixon's Revenge and "Buffy, Buffy Come Back To Me" by Angel and the Reruns.

Olsen, born in 1961 in Santa Monica, California, got her start as Cindy on *The Brady Bunch* in 1969. Those ever present ponytail curls were clearly inspired by Anissa Jones's look on *Family Affair*, although Olsen's cute lisp was all her own.

The two went in very different directions after their family friendly TV sitcoms concluded. Olsen, a single mom who spent 10 years as a graphic designer and has also worked in Los Angeles radio, has no history of drug abuse and no run-ins with the law. Nonetheless, she seems to have been dragged by association into the child stars gone wrong vortex.

Part of the confusion might spring from a 1976 NBC TV movie that premiered about a month after Jones's death was reported. *Dawn: Portrait of a Teenage Runaway*, directed by Randal Kleiser (Blue Lagoon), starred Olsen's

Brady-mate Eve Plumb as a 15-year-old who winds up a prostitute on Hollywood's mean streets.

Even though it was Plumb and not Olsen in the title role, the Jones/Olsen youngest child in pigtail connection must have all blurred into one more lost child star for many viewers. And while there was some confusion about Olsen and Jones and which one had died from a drug overdose, an entirely different death rumor also dogs the Brady girl. One urban legend had it that Olsen was dragged to her death after her coat got jammed in the door of a bus. Olsen told *TV Guide* in 1999 that that sprang from a real-life tragedy that happened to someone with a similar name.

At least Olsen appears to have a sense of humor about her grim associations. "I always liked being rumored to be dead, because it put me in company with, like Paul McCartney," Olsen told *TV Guide*. "If you watch one of the *Brady Bunch* episodes backwards, you can hear Greg saying, 'I buried Cindy.'"

Still another Olsen rumor, mentioned at Former Child Star Central, suggests the baby Brady went on to become a porn star. There are at least two associations to that. One, Olsen once played an X-rated actress on a 1983 episode of *Divorce Court*. The other is that Olsen bears a striking resemblance to an adult film star who appeared in the 1986 X-rated effort *Crocodile Blondee*. Crikey!

RUMOR: Full House's Jodie Sweetin died of a drug overdose.

FALSE: Overshadowed by her more ubiquitous costars, Olsen twins Mary-Kate and Ashley, Sweetin seems to have been caught up in the "out of sight, must be dead" rumor mill.

Then again, there's a "there but for the grace of other child stars" element of truth to this one. Born in 1982, the blonde-haired Los Angeles native costarred for eight seasons as middle sis Stephanie Tanner on the *Three Men and a Baby*–like family sitcom *Full House* (1987–95). Bob Saget, John Stamos, and Dave Coulier also starred on the series. Sweetin's career started when she was cast in a hot dog commercial at the tender age of four. At 13, after a successful series run, she found herself out of work and pretty much dropped out of the acting profession, concentrating on high school and college. She just wanted to blend in and have a normal life, she would later state.

That's when rumors of her death started to circulate. "Sometimes when somebody recognizes me, they are like, 'You're alive!' " she was once quoted as saying. "I don't know why people thought I was dead. I guess that's what happens when you make a life for yourself outside of Hollywood."

Or it is what people say to you after it has been reported in the tabloids that you've been on a three day drug bender. Sweetin didn't completely escape her child star celebrity unscathed. Married and divorced before she was 25, she appeared on *Good Morning America* in February of 2006 to talk about her two year addiction to crystal meth. She also admitted that she started experimenting with alcohol at 13.

A speed bender in March of 2005 was so acute, it put her in the hospital and forced her to confront her addiction. She entered rehab for six weeks. As she told *Good Morning America*, former cast members, including Stamos, Saget, and the Olsens, staged an intervention.

Sweetin now claims she's been clean and sober since early 2005. She gives lectures at schools against the dangers of drug abuse. "I'm lucky to be alive," she told students at Georgia Highlands College. "I'm very fortunate to be sober and be here today to tell my story."

RUMOR: Saved by the Bell's *Mark-Paul Gosselaar (Zack) and Mario Lopez (Slater) died in a car accident.*

FALSE: Did these two former child actors die of embarrassment when news hit in 2006 that former castmate Dustin Diamond (Screech) had released an amateur porn video? That would be yes. Did they die in a car accident? Uh, no.

Saved by the Bell was one of the most popular teen sitcoms of the '90s. The original NBC series, which was set at a Pacific Palisades, California, high school, ran from 1989 to 1993 and spawned two spin-offs, including *Saved by the Bell: The College Years* (1993-94). That one also featured Gosselaar, Lopez, and Diamond. Elizabeth Berkley and Tiffani Thiessen were two other prominent *Saved by the Bell* grads.

Several of the young actors and actresses on the series had rabid fan followings. They were constantly visible on teen magazine covers and high school locker walls, especially in the early '90s.

The idea that two of the stars had suddenly died seems to speak to some obsessive level of fan interest in this series. It sounds like a chorus right out of another generation's "Teen Angel"-type sob song. If you believe the Internet rumors, Gosselaar supposedly died in a car accident, a motorcycle crash, from a shark attack or a drug overdose. Another case of fans willing to believe the worst about an ex-child star. Internet sources suggest this one started spreading among high school and college campuses as early as the spring of 1994, thereby explaining why *Saved by the Bell: The College Years* was canceled.

The rumor might have been fueled by the 1998 movie *Dead Man on Campus*, which starred Gosselaar and Tom Everett Scott as two college roommates who party away their grades. When they learn of a college loop-hole that awards an "A" to roommates who have lost a mate, they search the campus for a suitable suicide victim.

Still, no one saw *Dead Man on Campus* (a break for both Gosselaar and Scott). Gosselaar went on to star opposite Dennis Franz for several seasons as detective John Clark in *NYPD Blue* and later with Geena Davis in the short-lived ABC drama *Commander in Chief*. In 2006, Lopez danced his way back into the spotlight, emerging as runner-up on the third installment of ABC's reality hit *Dancing with the Stars*.

The other thing about *Saved by the Bell* is that you either loved it or you hated it. Before it was taken down, one notorious website asked people to name the character they would most like to see killed off on a TV series. Characters on *Saved by the Bell* drew tens of thousands of votes. For some, it seems, no more Zack or Slater was pure wish fulfillment.

Happily married with two young children, Gosselaar addressed all the rumors on a 1998 press junket to promote *Dead Man on Campus*. "There's a rumor that I'm dead or I'm dying or whatever, these great rumors that I'm a drug addict, that I'm gay," he said. "It doesn't bother me. Whatever they say, it's fine by me. It doesn't affect my personal life."

CHAPTER 4

Lucy, You've Got Some 'Splainin' to Do: A Couple of Persistent *I Love Lucy* Myths

It was no rumor or myth—everybody loved Lucy. Besides being a gifted comedienne, Lucille Ball, who died at the age of 77 in 1989, was the First Lady of television, arguably the person who had the most impact with audiences in the history of the medium. *TV Guide* once wrote that the zany redhead "had a face seen by more people, more often, than the face of any other human being who ever lived."

I Love Lucy (1951–57) was responsible for several firsts. It was TV's first enduring hit (finishing number one in the ratings for four of its six seasons), the first Hollywood-based comedy, the first rerun, the first series regularly seen by over 10 million people, the first series filmed for broadcast (and not done live and later "telecined"), the first cover of *TV Guide.*

Lucille Ball and her Cuban-born bandleader hubby Desi Arnaz were also, in many ways, the first family of television. Tabloids and fan magazines of the day were filled with stories about their rocky marriage and frequent rumors about their offscreen blowups. Their 1960 divorce was a separation keenly felt across North America. That crazy marriage was one myth Americans never wanted to see shattered. After all, the show was called *I Love Lucy.* It was sad to see it end.

It wasn't all bad, though. Lucy and Desi had a lot of laughs and left a lot of laughs. *I Love Lucy*'s ultimate "first" might be that it showed that life goes on after a divorce, even if it is only in endless reruns.

As for spawning rumors, myths, and urban legends, Lucy might not have been first, but she sure was original.

RUMOR: *Radio transmissions picked up on Lucille Ball's dental fillings led to the capture of Japanese spies.*

UNSUBSTANTIATED: *Some rumors get started by overzealous publicists looking to grab a little ink for their clients, some by malicious corporate rivals looking to knock a competitor's product off the shelf, and others by bored kids high on soft drinks and Pop Rocks.*

This one was started by Lucille Ball.

Long before she became TV's number one star, Ball enjoyed a movie career that saw her go from chorus girl to B-movie queen and even starring roles opposite the likes of Bob Hope, Red Skelton, and the Marx Brothers.

It was while she was shooting *DuBarry Was a Lady*, a 1942 MGM release starring Skelton and Gene Kelly, that Ball started telling this crazy story about her dental work.

Sometime early in 1942, Ball had several temporary lead fillings placed in her teeth. One night, as she drove home from the MGM Studios in Los Angeles to the ranch she shared in the San Fernando Valley with husband Desi Arnaz, she said she heard strange music coming from her car radio. Except, as she soon discovered, her car radio was off. "The music kept getting louder and louder," she told confidant Jim Brochu (author of the Ball biography *Lucy in the Afternoon*), "and then I realized it was coming from my mouth."

Ball thought she was losing her mind and went to bed that night without telling anyone about the incident. The next day at the studio, however, she described what she had experienced to Buster Keaton. (The great silent comedian was making a living punching up scripts at the time—including Skelton's role on *DuBarry Was a Lady*.) It was Keaton who apparently suggested to Ball—perhaps in jest—that she was picking up radio signals through the fillings in her teeth. The same thing happened to a friend of his, he told her.

About a week later, Ball took a different route home from the studio. More strange sounds started emanating from her mouth, although this time, instead of music, Ball claimed she heard tapping. It sounded to her like Morse code.

Ball stopped by the MGM security gate the next day and reported the experience. "They called the FBI or something," Ball told Brochu. This led, she claimed, to the area in Coldwater Canyon near the route she took home being searched. "Sure enough," Ball told Brochu, "they found an underground Japanese radio station. It was somebody's gardener, but sure enough, they were spies."

The story also appears in W. G. Harris' book, *Lucy and Desi: The Legendary Love Story of Television's Most Famous Couple*. In that account, a secret radio transmitter was discovered in a tool shed belonging to a Japanese gardener. The man was busted for being a member of a west coast spy ring.

Sounds like a crazy scheme straight out of *I Love Lucy*, doesn't it? The story did wind up, not in a TV show, but in a play, the Cole Porter musical *Something for the Boys*, which came out in 1943. Ball had told the story to Ethel Merman in 1942 and Merman apparently passed it on to Porter.

America's entry into World War II, which had begun with the attack on Pearl Harbor on December 7, 1941, had many California residents fearing another surprise attack. Japanese Americans had begun to be rounded up and put in relocation camps. Ball would have been mindful and perhaps a little fearful at the time.

Enough to believe she was a human antenna? There have been documented reports of radio broadcasts being transmitted through dental fillings, as well as shrapnel fragments embedded in the skulls of Vietnam War veterans.

The TV show *MythBusters* decided to test the Radio Free Lucy theory to see if it had any merit. They interviewed Brochu, a confidant of Ball's during her later years, who told them the actress was of sound mind and at no other time ever complained of hearing voices in her head. (Except maybe Ricky screaming, "LOOOCIE!") They determined that the radio station near Ball's route home from MGM was a 50,000 watt station, and there was quite a bit of clay in the soil in that area which would help amplify the signal.

The two hosts of *MythBusters*, Adam Savage and Jamie Hyneman, tested the theory using human skulls fitted with different types of fillings. Then they tracked down some vintage radio equipment to send the signals. When they couldn't pick up any electrical activity in the teeth, they declared the myth busted.

Savage and Hyneman also deconstructed Ball's other claim to hearing Morse code in her mouth. They figured Ball was experiencing a galvanic reaction, which apparently occurs when two dissimilar metals in the mouth mix with saliva, allowing a small amount of current to build and discharge. This could give the impression that a person was hearing something like Morse code in their head.

The *MythBusters* experimented with two different kinds of fillings and then set them in a vinegar solution. The level of acidity, they figured, would make for an excellent conductor and would approximate the level of acidity in saliva after eating.

A small amount of current was detected. So, in theory, it was possible for Ball to have experienced what she claims to have heard inside her own mouth. The *MythBusters*, however, also gained access to Ball's FBI file. There they found no mention of her involvement in capturing a Japanese radio spy, so they declared this myth busted, too.

Still, why would Ball have made either of these stories up? Many stars love attention, but Ball certainly wasn't looking to establish a reputation as a kook.

She may have been trying, however, to shore up her reputation as a patriot. The *MythBusters* show interviewed a lecturer on Japanese espionage who had been with the FBI during World War II. Professor Rusty Oapps said Japanese soldiers did make a few tentative attacks on American soil during the war, including dropping bombs from high altitude balloons and firing rounds into petrol tank farms from submarines. On February 23, 1942, for example, a Japanese submarine was spotted off the coast of California near Santa Barbara.

Folklorist Heather Joseph Witham was also interviewed. She spoke about how people dealt with their fear of Japanese raids and suggested that the idea of Lucy foiling a plot brought comfort to many Americans. If they couldn't outwit the zany redhead, some might have figured, they couldn't fool the rest of us.

Still, Lucy in the early '40s was not the enormous star she was in the early '50s. That's when her reputation really needed a little patriotic push. Which brings us to...

RUMOR: *Lucille Ball was once a member of the Communist Party.*

TRUE: *If you were reading the above story carefully (and why wouldn't you be?), you might have wondered why in the world there was an FBI file on America's favorite comedienne.*

The height of *I Love Lucy*'s popularity in the '50s coincided with a great deal of fear and paranoia about the perceived rise of communism in America. The Cold War, the Red Scare, and *I Love Lucy* all helped define the decade.

Ball was called before the House Un-American Activities Committee (HUAC) on two separate occasions to answer charges that she had once joined the Communist party. Ball had, in fact, signed up in 1936 at the urging of her grandfather, Fred Hunt, a socialist union man and always a bit of a radical. She appeared before HUAC and told them that she and her brother signed Communist membership cards simply to please the older man. "In those days, that was not a big terrible thing to do," she told the committee. "It was almost as terrible to be a Republican in those days."

Ball added that she had never voted Communist in an election. She swore a statement into the record: "I am not a Communist now. I never have been. I never wanted to be. Nothing in the world could ever change my mind."

Ball was dismissed from the HUAC sessions and felt assured her testimony would remain confidential. That weekend, however, her world was turned upside down when popular radio commentator Walter Winchell blurted a blind item that "the top television comedienne has been confronted with her membership in the Communist Party."

A week or so later the local *Los Angeles Herald Express* ran the headline "LUCILLE BALL A RED." Ball and Arnaz and their publicists sprang into full damage control. To get the word out fast, Arnaz told gossip columnist Hedda Hopper that "the only thing red about Lucy is her hair, and even that is not legitimate."

Arnaz used the line again when introducing his wife to their studio audience at the next taping following news of the scandal. She got a standing ovation and when *I Love Lucy* remained at the top of the ratings, it was clear Lucy had been forgiven by the only committee that mattered—viewers—and that the crisis had passed. The couple were also cleared by FBI director J. Edgar Hoover, invited to the White House, and absolved in the media. Even Winchell backpedaled: "Tonight," he told his radio listeners, "Mr. Lincoln is drying his tears for making her go through this." (Winchell himself, of course, took none of the blame.)

Ball later acknowledged that if news of her Communist card signing had broken four or five years earlier—before *I Love Lucy* had become so incredibly popular and when the Hollywood witch hunt was at an unstoppable pitch—her career would have been ruined.

The episode also adds context to the previous rumor about the fillings and the Japanese spy story. Ball had every reason to want to promote herself as an all-American patriot by the time the HUAC report leaked. Yet that dental rumor predated the Red Lucy scare by 10 years. Still, the question must be asked: why didn't Ball's fillings warn her not to sign that Communist Party card?

RUMOR: I Love Lucy costar Vivian Vance was contractually obligated to remain at least 20 pounds overweight.

FALSE: While this story has been told by almost everyone associated with the show over the years, there is no evidence such a contract demand was ever in place. Vance, of course, played neighbor and landlady Ethel Mertz on I Love Lucy *(1951–57), the wildly popular sitcom starring husband and wife Desi Arnaz and Lucille Ball.*

Vance was appearing as a hooker with a heart of gold in a play titled *The Voice of the Turtle* when producer Arnaz, at the urging of his director, caught her performance at the La Jolla Playhouse. By the first intermission Arnaz was convinced he had found his Ethel. Still, he had to sell his movie star wife on Vance.

Ball had wanted her friend Bea Benaderet (later the voice of Betty Rubble on *The Flintstones*, as well as a regular on *Petticoat Junction*) for the part, but that actress was already committed to *The Burns & Allen Show*. Ball had never heard of Vance and greeted her coolly on the first day of rehearsals, basically telling the New Mexico native that she didn't look like a landlady. "I want a dumpy, fat woman in a chenille bathrobe and furry slippers with curlers in her hair," she told Vance. "You got her," snapped back Vance, saying that was how she looked first thing in the morning.

Arnaz had to break things up and move along the rehearsals. Ball had to draw in her nails and eventually concede that Vance had the chops. Even though she was just two years older than Ball, Vance, who died in 1979, had to look older teamed with William Frawley. The veteran character actor was more than 20 years her senior and looked all of it as Ethel's crabby husband, Fred Mertz.

Vance usually did look frumpier than Ball on the series. Her character was usually dressed in plain cotton dresses and her hair and makeup did nothing to make her look any younger.

Her weight did fluctuate during the series, but that had nothing to do, apparently, with any contract stipulation. Vance, in fact, kept trying to lose weight.

The writers often had Fred take cheap shots at Ethel's weight on the show. It was part of the character's shtick, but it sometimes bordered on meanness. Vance, apparently, felt that she could never let her weight get too out of hand because then those jokes would no longer be accepted by the audience. "If my husband in this series makes fun of my weight and I'm actually fat, then the audience won't laugh," she reasoned, "they'll feel sorry for me. But if he calls me 'fat old bag' and I'm not heavy, then it will seem funny."

The rumor of a weight rider in Vance's contract may have been set off as a result of a joke. As relayed in Frank Castelluccio and Alvin Walker's *The*

Other Side of Ethel Mertz, the two actresses were at a party where Ball gave Vance a bogus contract that stipulated she gain five pounds a week, not wear fake eyelashes and not dye her hair within five shades of Ball's fiery red locks. Another joke rider insisted that Vance not get as many laughs as Lucy.

When Vance was hired to appear on Ball's next sitcom, *The Lucy Show* (1962–68), she was the one who insisted on a stipulation in her contract. Vance asked for more glamorous clothes and that her character be named Vivian; she was tired of people calling her Ethel.

CHAPTER 5

Set Phasers for Stun: Some Enterprising *Star Trek* Legends

If Lucy still has some 'splainin' to do, *Star Trek* has been 'splained to death. The sci-fi series has been more dissected and deconstructed than the final few minutes of *The Sopranos*.

More popular in reruns than it ever was during its three seasons on NBC (1966–69), the franchise-spawning sci-fi drama never ranked beyond number 52 in the annual ratings. Long-forgotten shows such as *Iron Horse* and *Mr. Terrific* drew bigger audiences in 1967.

Fans of the show, and they are legion, know all the backstory by now. The series was created by Gene Roddenberry, the head writer for a popular '60s western called *Have Gun, Will Travel*. He pitched *Star Trek* to NBC as a space western, or, "*Wagon Train* to the stars." The most famous *Star Trek* character, Captain James T. Kirk, wasn't even in the original pilot, which featured Jeffrey Hunter as the skipper. Most of the familiar faces from the Enterprise's flight deck, in fact, were not in that expensive pilot, which was rejected by the network.

Fortunately, a second pilot was shot. Hunter was tied up with another gig, so William Shatner—who once turned down the role of Dr. Kildare—became Kirk. He joined Leonard Nimoy, who played pointy-eared Vulcan Spock on both pilots, and the two went warp speed into TV history.

And on and on it boldly goes. The series spawned four long-running spin-offs, including *Star Trek: The Next Generation*, as well as nearly a dozen feature films. Like other pop culture phenomena, it also inspired an intense fan following, a cult-like stature, and several persistent rumors, urban myths, and legends.

One involves the phrase most often associated with the show. Just as Humphrey Bogart never said, "Play it again, Sam," in *Casablanca* and Cary Grant never said, "Judy, Judy, Judy," in any film, no one in any of the 79 original episodes of *Star Trek* ever once said, "Beam me up, Scotty." It was always "Two to beam up, Mr. Scott," or something like that. As Spock would (and did) say, "Fascinating."

Here are a few other *Star Trek* rumors and myths that deserve a second look.

RUMOR: *Ensign Chekov was written into the second season of* Star Trek *after an editorial in the Communist daily newspaper* Pravda *chided the sci-fi series for not having a Soviet crew member aboard the starship* Enterprise.

UNSUBSTANTIATED: *At first blush, as Spock would also say, this sounds "highly illogical." Why would the Soviet government's main propaganda organ care what happened on a poorly-rated American space opera? But there is some evidence to suggest that* Star Trek *executive producer and creator Gene Roddenberry did react to an outside suggestion that he diversify his flight deck.*

The most successful sci-fi franchise ever premiered to so-so ratings in September of 1966. The series already had a fairly diverse (especially by 1966 standards) cast. Besides Captain Kirk (Canadian-born actor William Shatner), there was an African American female communications officer (Lt. Uhura, played by Nichelle Nichols), an Asian flight control officer (Lt. Sulu, George Takei), and, well, Scotty (James Doohan). And, of course, a Vulcan first officer (Spock, Leonard Nimoy).

Still, that was the twenty-third century. Back in the mid-twentieth century, the Soviet Union was the only rival to the United States in the real space race. Where was the Enterprise's Russian cosmonaut?

Early in the series' run, Roddenberry had already decided to add to his cast. In a memo to casting director Joe D'Agosta dated September 22, 1966, he suggested a "young, irreverent, English-accented 'Beatle' type" be added to the show, "Like the smallish fellow who looks to be a hit on *The Monkees*." Roddenberry found his Davy Jones in Walter Koenig, who wore a mop top wig for a few *Star Trek* episodes until his real hair grew in like a Monkee. Yet, by the time he was introduced on the show at the beginning of season two, the character had transformed from a Brit teen idol to a Russian-accented ensign named Pavel Chekov.

According to the editors of *Entertainment Weekly*'s "The 100 Greatest TV Shows of All Time," "The show's spin doctors insisted that he was hired because the Russian newspaper *Pravda* complained that an international space station was incomplete without a Russian on board."

Indeed, that's the reason given in *The Making of Star Trek*, the official companion book published during the original network run of the series. Roddenberry is quoted as saying omitting a Russian at the beginning "was a major error on our part," and that he had written "a long, polite letter to the minister of cultural affairs in Moscow, apologizing for the error and telling him about Chekov."

As Desilu vice president Herb Solow later explained, this was apparently in response to an article in *Pravda* criticizing *Star Trek* for being "typically capitalistic" in omitting a comrade. Solow went on to say that Roddenberry, always keen to promote diversity and peaceful coexistence on television, warmed to the idea immediately.

Trouble is, no one can find that original *Pravda* editorial. As Snopes.com points out, Roddenberry himself claims he never saw it and that he was just told about it by an actor on the show toward the end of 1966.

The actor certainly wasn't Shatner, who dismissed the whole *Pravda* deal as trumped up nonsense in his book, *Star Trek Memories*. "Here's the truth," writes Shatner. "This long-established, widely believed bit of *Star Trek* history is entirely false, and was simply the product of an overzealous public relations department."

George Takei has another take, which also seems to shoot down the *Pravda* theory. "I'll tell you what the truth of this is," Takei told me early in 2007 as he was preparing to join the cast of NBC's new sci-fi hit *Heroes*. Takei says he lobbied Roddenberry and the writers to beef up his part. "The first season, I wanted Sulu do be able to do more." Roddenberry agreed, promising to feature Sulu starting at the beginning of the second season. As a show of good faith, Roddenberry even forwarded Takei the scripts so he could see that his part had been given a boost.

Takei, however, got bogged down shooting *The Green Berets* with John Wayne during the hiatus between *Star Trek*'s first and second seasons. When that film shoot dragged on into the *Star Trek* schedule, Takei says Roddenberry was forced to hire another actor—Walter Koenig—and give his new character the lines intended for Takei. "I had those lines memorized!" complains Takei. "After all my hard lobbying, all my hard work, this guy comes in from nowhere and takes my scenes! Those were my words Chekov was muttering. I hated Walter before I even met him!"

To add insult to injury, Takei says he had to share his dressing room with Koenig after he returned to the set. "That made me hate him even more," jokes Takei, who says his hatred turned to pity "for the poor actor who had to wear that wig." Today the two actors are good friends.

Seems logical, then, that there is nothing to the *Pravda* story beyond a little creative public relations (PR) spinning. One nagging little loose end, however. As reproduced in Solow and associate producer Robert Justman's 1996 book, *Inside Star Trek: The Real Story*, Roddenberry did write a letter to the editor of *Pravda* in 1967 informing him that Chekov had been added to the crew. Could this too have simply been a little PR backpedaling?

The 2006 TV special *Star Trek 40 Years* dismissed the rumor, suggesting that no one in the Soviet Union was even aware of *Star Trek* in 1966/67 and that spirited young Chekov was simply added to give the show more youth appeal. So what about the report that suggests a *Pravda* reporter caught an episode of *Star Trek* in Germany? Until someone can beam up the original *Pravda* story, this rumor will boldly go unsolved until the twenty-third century.

RUMOR: *The ashes of* Star Trek *engineer Montgomery "Scotty" Scott (James Doohan) were blasted into suborbital space.*

TRUE: *One to beam up, Captain. Doohan, born in Canada of Irish—not Scottish—descent, passed away on July 20, 2005, the 37th anniversary of the first manned moon landing. Coincidence? We think not.*

The actor who played the Enterprise's crusty chief engineer lived to be 85. His last months were plagued by the onset of Alzheimer's and Parkinson's disease. In accordance with his wishes, he was cremated, and a lipstick-sized vial of some of his ashes were blasted into space on a rocket launched on April 28, 2007.

The ashes of over 200 people, representing 10 nations, were also on board a SpaceLoft XL rocket for that last ride, which took off from New Mexico. The outer space salute is part of a memorial service offered by a Texas-based company called Celestis. The remains of Mercury astronaut Gordon Cooper also made the trip.

Others have boldly made the ash dash before. The remains of Dr. Timothy Leary, the psychedelic drug doctor who passed away in 1996, got blasted in 1997, as did what was left of *Star Trek* creator Gene Roddenberry (who died in 1991). This may not have been the first time Roddenberry and Leary got high together, but we'll leave that to the next rumor book.

It's not the first time Doohan made history, either. During the second World War, he took part in the allied invasion of Normandy, hitting Juno

Beach as a member of the Royal Canadian Artillery. He and his unit were attacked by enemy fire, with Doohan struck by four bullets. The middle finger of his right hand was shot off, and a bullet hit him in the chest. Only a silver cigarette case in his breast pocket, a gift from his brother, saved his life.

When he began acting in Canada in the '50s, he became acquainted with future *Star Trek* skipper William Shatner, a native of Montreal. When I spoke with him in Los Angeles shortly after Doohan's death in 2005, Shatner told me that he was the one who brought Doohan to the attention of the *Star Trek* producers. "I think I had a hand—if not being instrumental—in bringing him on the set," he said. Shatner recalled Doohan as one of Canada's "top radio actors," with a rich voice that he used to full advantage to create memorable accents and characters.

Still, Doohan didn't always have good things to say about Shatner. "Jimmy had some issues with me," Shatner acknowledged. "I don't understand them, but that was the way he was." What exactly was it that bugged Doohan about his former Enterprise skipper? Shatner shrugged and recalled Doohan being quoted once as saying something like, "I don't remember, but it must be something."

As for his own mortal remains, Shatner hasn't indicated if he wants to follow Scotty into space. He did turn down a chance to ride into orbit while still alive. Brit billionaire Sir Richard Branson offered Shatner a seat on the inaugural voyage of the VSS Enterprise in 2008, scheduled to lift off from the same base where Scotty's ashes went into orbit. That's a $215,000 ticket. Sigourney Weaver, who starred in the sci-fi *Alien* movie adventures, has accepted a similar offer.

Shatner was quoted as saying, "I'm interested in man's march into the unknown, but to vomit in space is not my idea of a good time."

"Neither," he added, "is a fiery crash with the vomit hovering over me."

RUMOR: *TV's first interracial kiss was between Captain James T. Kirk and Lt. Uhura on Star Trek.*

FALSE: *Set phasers for stun! Every Trekker in the galaxy knows Kirk and Uhura (Nichelle Nichols) engaged in TV's first interracial lip lock. It's right there in the Captain's log, as well as about 900 books written about the sci-fi series.*

The episode is called "Plato's Stepchildren," from the third and final season. Stardate, or at least, airdate, November 22, 1968.

The episode was pretty out there, even by '60s sci-fi TV standards. After they beam down on a strange planet called "Platonious," Captain Kirk and several of his Enterprise crew members are captured by the locals. They covet Dr. McCoy (DeForest Kelley) and want him to attend to their ailing leader. They try to keep the Enterprise crew on their planet by using their superior willpower, forcing Kirk, Spock, and the others to dress up in goofy Roman Empire–era togas and gowns and perform for their amusement.

Things get a little sadistic and kinky as the aliens try to humiliate Kirk and the others. Kirk and Spock are forced to fight each other. Spock is forced to sing a sappy love song. Fortunately, no one forces Kirk to sing "Mr. Tambourine Man" (a song Shatner reduced to a camp classic on his 1968 vanity album *The Transformed Man*)—that would have been too sadistic.

The Platonian leaders then try to force Kirk and Spock to make out with the human women, Uhura and Christine. At one point, things get extra kinky as the two men take up whips, which they snap at the earth babes.

That's when the Platonians try to will Kirk into kissing Uhura. Since Kirk was always eager to make out with just about anything in a skirt through-out the run of the series, and Uhura was a stunner, this would not seem to be such an arm twister. But this was 1968, with racial violence raging in the streets of America in the wake of the assassination of Dr. Martin Luther King. Despite a decade of civil rights advances, there were still some places you just didn't boldly go on American network TV.

Just the same, Kirk and Uhura move in for the embrace, but if you watch very closely, their lips do not actually touch. Shatner turns his face slightly at the last moment. (Kirk and Spock had secretly taken an antidote that eventually allowed them to resist the mind control.) What we really have here is TV's first interracial air kiss.

There is evidence that the network and/or the producers felt an inter-racial kiss was still too much of a hot potato in 1968. According to one account, there were suggestions from studio executives at Paramount during the shoot that Spock, instead of Kirk, should kiss Uhura to avoid alienating viewers watching in some Southern states. Who knew Vulcan/African American necking was so acceptable in the South?

It has also been reported that some NBC affiliates in the South refused to air the episode because of the interracial kiss. While that may be true, no one at NBC could confirm this when this scenario was put to them in 2007.

In her 1994 autobiography, *Beyond Uhura: Star Trek and Other Memories*, Nichols notes that NBC did hear from Southern viewers over the kissing scene (suggesting, of course, that it did air in at least some Southern markets). Her memory is that the response was much more positive than the network had feared. "I am totally opposed to the mixing of the races," one white Southerner wrote, according to Nichols. "However, any time a red-blooded

American boy like Captain Kirk gets a beautiful dame on his arms that looks like Uhura, he ain't gonna fight it."

What is ironic is that no one at the time seemed to have a problem with what seems truly objectionable about the episode today—that sexual assault aspect of the forced seduction through mind control.

Shatner himself maintains that, because of the controversy at the time, two versions of the scene were shot, one where he and Nichols actually kiss and one where they just come close. It is that second take that made the original cut and was the only shot ever shown in reruns.

The episode was one of a handful of *Star Trek* hours banned from British TV screens. "Plato's Stepchildren" was not shown in the United Kingdom until December 22, 1993, but not because of the Kirk/Uhura kiss. (An interracial couple had been puckering up on British screens as early as 1964 on the prime time soap *Emergency Ward 10*.) British censors simply found the episode too sadistic, or maybe they were just creeped out when the Platonian dwarf named Alexander jumped on Kirk and mounted him like a horse. Whoa.

Turns out the kissing color barrier had also been crossed on U.S. TV screens about a year before Kirk and Uhura's celebrated non-smooch. Sammy Davis, Jr., and Nancy Sinatra kissed each other on the December 1967 variety special *Movin' with Nancy*.

Still, as the old saying goes, why let truth stand in the way of a good story. Nichols and Shatner continue to get mileage out of their Platonian pseudo pucker. In August of 2006, when Nichols was a guest on Comedy Central's raunchy roast of Shatner, Nichols looked at her former costar—who apparently wasn't too popular on the *Star Trek* set—and said, "Let's make history again...and you can kiss my black ass!"

RUMOR: The Star Trek *theme has lyrics.*

TRUE: Just as there really are lyrics to the Bonanza *theme—another bit of music familiar to classic TV fans strictly as an instrumental—there really are lyrics to Star Trek's soaring opening theme. How they came about, however, is a sour note in this space saga.*

Now, it is important to state that the lyrics were never sung on the show. Viewers were never subjected to not-so-golden-throats William Shatner or Leonard Nimoy singing from the bridge of the Enterprise.

What everyone does remember are those first four notes, Shatner's stirring, "Space...the final frontier..." narration, and then the soaring orchestral theme (called "Where No Man Has Gone Before"). It was composed by veteran Hollywood arranger Alexander Courage.

In other words, it took Courage to write that theme. Okay, we got that out of the way.

Courage's credits run all the way back to the great MGM musicals of the '50s. As an orchestrator/arranger, he worked on everything from *Show Boat* and *The Band Wagon* to *Superman*, *The Poseidon Adventure*, and *Jurassic Park*.

In terms of TV shows, Courage also served as a composer on *Lost in Space*, *Voyage to the Bottom of the Sea*, *The Waltons*, and *Daniel Boone* (although he did not write those themes, but music heard during the episodes).

Never much of a sci-fi fan, dismissing the genre as "marvelous malarkey," he set out to write some malarkey music to go with the images. "Little did I know when I wrote that first A flat for the flute that it was going to go down in history," he said in the 2004 documentary *The Masters behind the Musicals*.

Inspired by the old standard, "Beyond the Blue Horizon," Courage came up with something for flute, organ, vibraphone, and soprano. Creator Gene Roddenberry heard it and ordered the soprano part beefed up. As Courage explains, "He wanted to hear the girl more, because he was such a sex maniac." It seems that, not unlike *Star Trek*'s romantic hero, Captain Kirk, Roddenberry has the sex drive of a Klingon.

If Courage sounds a little bitter, well, I'm getting to that.

When NBC picked up *Star Trek* for its 1966 to 1967 season, Courage stood to make money every time an episode ran. About a year into the run of the show, he noticed his royalty check had been cut in half. What gives, he asked the producer.

That's when he discovered that Roddenberry had hastily penned lyrics to the theme, allowing him to lay claim to half the performance royalties as a cocomposer. It didn't matter that there was never any intention to record the lyrics or ever use them on the show. Roddenberry got half.

Courage tried to argue that Roddenberry's little ploy was unethical. Nonetheless, it was legal. Roddenberry had Courage's signature on a contract clearly allowing lyrics to be added later and for the compensation to be split. It was no accident Roddenberry's spaceship was called Enterprise.

Joel Engel's 1994 book *Gene Roddenberry: The Myth and the Man behind Star Trek*, portrays the producer as a bit of a glory hound. He also apparently felt that *Star Trek* would never be a money maker and that he had to grab whatever cash he could. "Hey, I have to get money somewhere," he told Courage. "I'm sure not going to get it out of the profits of *Star Trek*."

CHAPTER 6

The Naked Truth: They Don't Call It the "Boob Tube" for Nothing

Okay, admit it, you skipped all that *Tonight Show* and *I Love Lucy* stuff and went straight for this chapter. Shame on you. Go back and read those other chapters and come back here later.

Okay, you are back. Feel better, don't you? It is good to read books in order. Now, get your mind back in the gutter.

TV and nudity have been making headlines long before Janet Jackson had her top ripped open by Justin Timberlake during that Super Bowl XXXVIII halftime show. When you get to the game shows chapter (okay, tell me you didn't skip ahead to that one, too), you'll read how one excited contestant really did let her halter top "come on down" as she ran down the aisle toward Bob Barker on *The Price Is Right.*

Here are two stories about three other boobs: Madonna and Scott Baio.

RUMOR: You can see Madonna's bare breast in her "Pappa Don't Preach" video.

TRUE: Here's a shocker: Madonna's right breast has been seen by millions of people.

Alert the media. This is right up there with "nerds seen at *Star Trek* convention."

The pop princess has been waving her ta-tas at cameras since first making the scene in the mid-80s. A shrewd businesswoman, Madonna always knew how to shake her moneymaker and grow rich off controversies both real and imagined. Whether she was squeezing them into cone-shaped bras or exposing them in her infamous *Sex* book, Madonna always kept her breasts in front of her music.

But even she didn't intend to bust the bare boob barrier as early in her career as she did. In the 1986 video for "Pappa Don't Preach," Madonna can be seen dancing up a storm in a barely there bustier. At one point, she throws her arms high in the air, exposing her fabulous right breast.

It happens so fast, hardly anyone ever notices. The director of the video, James Foley (*Glengarry Glen Ross*), told *TV Guide* in 1999 that he did not spot the slip until his eagle-eyed editor paused Madonna's wayward mammary in mid-freeze frame. "Both of us said, 'Uh-oh,'" recalled Foley, who toyed with not even telling the singer before deciding he had better give her the head's up. Madonna's reaction was predictable: "Yeah, so? What's the problem?" she told Foley, who was relieved. It was her best dance sequence, he rationalized. Plus, he added, "It was a very pretty nipple."

Fifteen years later, America flipped its lid when Janet Jackson *didn't* expose all of her breast during a Super Bowl halftime show (a piece of jewelry covered her nipple). Stiff fines totaling more than half a million dollars were levied against CBS and a general censorship chill descended on broadcast television for at least a couple of years.

Yet when Madonna released what *TV Guide* jokingly referred to "the first pop-up video," there was no public outcry over the accidental nudity. Instead, some groups objected to the song's storyline, the tale of a pregnant teen who decides to keep her baby. Nudity? Nyet. Morality? For shame.

RUMOR: Joanie Loves Chachi *was the biggest TV hit ever in South Korea because "Chachi" is Korean for "penis."*

FALSE: Let's get one thing straight. Joanie Loves Chachi *was never a hit, in Korea or anywhere else. The ABC sitcom, a spin-off of the hit series* Happy Days, *starred Erin Moran and Scott Baio and had a 17-episode run during the 1982 to 1983 season.*

What is true is that "jaw-jee" is a Korean slang term for the male genitalia and the "ch" and "j" sounds are similar in that language. But *Joanie Loves Chachi* executive producer Garry Marshall's and Baio's claims that this made the show South Korea's highest-rated program is pretty farfetched.

The show did air in Korea in English, without subtitles (probably the best way to enjoy it), on the American Armed Forces Korean Network. It was never broadcast on regular South Korean TV (a great stroke of diplomacy), so there was no way it could have reached a huge audience there.

By the way, "Chachi" in English means "lame TV show."

CHAPTER 7

A Word from Our Sponsor: Rumors and Myths and Commercials

Here are some startling facts. According to the American Academy of Pediatrics, the average American child sees about 40,000 TV commercials a year. By the time we reach 65, most Americans will have seen 65.2 million commercials.

No wonder Mikey from those Life cereal ads of the '70s or Jared from the more recent Subway campaigns seem so familiar to us; we've seen these guys more often than some members of our own families.

It follows, then, that some of TV's most persistent rumors and urban legends center around characters or actors from the field of TV advertising. Ads, like rumors, thrive on repetition and exaggeration. Fantasy and hyperbole are their stock-in-trade. So is familiarity. The Maytag repairman or Pillsbury Dough Boy are as familiar to most TV viewers as the biggest stars of the highest-rated dramas or sitcoms.

Yet all we know about those ad icons is whatever can be crammed into a 30-second spot. Does the Man from Glad really wear white all the time, even on his day off around the house?

People magazine and others ran features on Clara Peller, the retired manicurist who bellowed, "Where's the beef?" in those Wendy's hamburger spots from the '80s. She went on to cut a "Where's the Beef?" single and even appeared in a low-budget movie before passing away at 86—just a few short years after she rose from obscurity to become a TV icon. Some ad personalities have their own Web sites and fan clubs. They are the embodiment of Andy Warhol's famous phrase that everyone will be famous for 15 minutes—even if it is only for 30 seconds at a time.

Some might even inspire a little envy or loathing. Sure, Jared lost all that weight eating Subway sandwiches—I heard it was gastric bypass surgery. Sure, little Mikey might be cute, what with those chubby cheeks and all, but the kid blew up real good eatin' them Pop Rocks and drinking that soda pop. Wait a minute—I thought Mikey hated everything. Maybe there's more to this kid than we know—or can imagine.

RUMOR: "Mikey," the kid from those Life cereal spots, died from eating Pop-Rocks and drinking soda.

FALSE: In 1971, a cute commercial for Quaker Oats' Life cereal premiered featuring three young tykes sitting at the breakfast table. Two of the boys refuse to dip into their new bowl of Life until finicky Mikey, who "hates everything," has a whiff. To their surprise, "He likes it!"

The spot ran until the mid-80s, and in 1999 it was ranked number 10 among TV Guide's "50 Greatest Commercials of All Time."

Those three kids in the commercial were all brothers in real life—the Gilchrists: John, Michael, and Tommy. But it was four-year-old John who stood out as ad icon Mikey—even though he doesn't say a word in the spot. And it was John Gilchrist—remembered simply as Mikey from those Life cereal ads—who supposedly died from eating Pop Rocks candy and drinking Coca-Cola.

"This is an example of a childhood bravery rumor," wrote Hal Morgan and Kerry Tucker in their 1984 book Rumor! Those authors felt that kids spread rumors like this to feel more courageous when they ate Pop Rocks.

The rumor spread throughout school yards for years—eating Pop Rocks and swallowing Coke creates a deadly fizz that blows out your stomach. Every kid knew it. Gilchrist, who went on to become a an account executive in the advertising department of CBS News Radio, told TV Guide in 1998 that he had no idea how the rumor got started. "But I remember the day I found out about it," he told the magazine. "I was 10 or 11 and my mom got a call from some woman in the Midwest saying she was really sorry to hear about what had happened to me." Gilchrist says his mom had no idea what the woman was talking about.

The rumor first spread throughout college campuses in the early '80s. The idea that something bad had happened to this kid must have seemed plausible to students who had grown up with the campaign. There was even a variation to the "Mikey is dead" rumor: that Gilchrist had choked to death after biting off the head of a G.I. Joe doll. (This sounds suspiciously like "Beaver died in Vietnam" territory.)

The Mikey rumor so unnerved General Foods, which manufactured Pop Rocks, that it mounted a counter propaganda campaign to stem the rumors. In 1979, they took out full-page ads in 45 major publications, wrote 50,000 letters to school principals, and sent the inventors of Pop Rocks across America to demonstrate that all Pop Rocks and Coke could do was make you burp.

When that failed to put the rumor to rest, General Foods stopped marketing Pop Rocks. As Snopes's rumor sleuth Barbara Mikkelson points out, consumers took that as proof that the product really was life threatening, or at least Life cereal threatening. In reality, Kraft Foods purchased the rights to Pop Rocks in the mid-80s and started marketing them under a different name (the über lame Action Candy) before switching back to Pop Rocks, which are still available today.

Conspiracy theorists also jumped all over the fact that when new Life cereal ads started to appear in 2000 showing a grown-up Mikey, it was eventually revealed that it wasn't Gilchrist behind the bowl but a new actor—Jimmy Starace—hired to play the grown-up Mikey. Why? Because, said the rumor mongers, the original Mikey was dead. Which, as Gilchrist pointed out to *TV Guide*, is a joke, or, as Mark Twain once said, at least an exaggeration. "To this day," said Gilchrist, "people think I'm dead."

As for the lethal Pop Rocks and soda can make you explode theory, this was debunked in the original pilot episode of the Discovery series *MythBusters*. The series tested the idea that little Mikey was challenged to eat six packs of Pop Rock candy and down six cans of soda. After tests were conducted near Albany, New York, at the Rensselaer Polytechnic Institute, risking the lives of hosts Adam Savage and Jamie Hyneman, the experts at *MythBusters* reached this conclusion: there was not enough carbon dioxide produced by the reaction of Pop Rocks and soda to make a stomach explode—but it could give you a tummy ache. Not even Mikey would like that.

Another TV show, however, may keep that exploding Pop Rocks and soda theory bubbling for years. On the sixth-season episode of *The Simpsons*, "Homer Badman," greedy Homer smashes a glass case and swipes a prized gummy version of the Venus de Milo. With security guards in hot pursuit, Homer karate kicks a soda machine, sending a can of "Buzz" cola into his outstretched hand. With the other hand he rips open a bag of "Pop Rox." Homer shakes the two together and hurls them at the approaching candy conventioneers. "See you in Hell, candy boys!" he shouts as giant balls of flames engulf the exploding convention hall. Take that, *MythBusters*. D'oh!

RUMOR: *Jared Fogle, the star of commercials for the Subway chain of sandwich stores, has died.*

FALSE: *For some people, the fact that Fogle lost weight from eating Subway sandwiches is just too hard to swallow. Fogle was a 20-year-old Indiana University student when he decided to do something about his bad eating habits. Beginning in March of 1998, the 425-pound Fogle began following a strict, 1,000 calories a day diet regimen which saw him skip breakfast (except for coffee), eat a six-inch turkey sub (hold the cheese, oil, and mayo) for lunch (plus a bag of Baked Lays chips), and a diet soda. For dinner, he downed a foot-long veggie sub, loaded with three kinds of peppers, extra veggies, and no cheese, all washed down with diet soft drinks.*

Eventually, when his weight began to decrease, Fogle introduced a little exercise into his routine, walking the one and a half miles a day to school instead of taking the bus. There wasn't much exercise involved in fetching lunch and dinner—he lived next door to the local Subway sandwich shop.

After three months, he lost 94 lbs. Within a year, he had dropped a whopping 245 lbs. His waist size shrank from 60 inches to 34. His weight eventually settled in at 190 pounds, perfect for his six foot two frame.

News of Fogle's remarkable "Subway diet" quickly spread. It started with a report in the *Indiana Daily Student*. The Associated Press jumped on the story. *Men's Health* even did a feature. That brought Fogle to the attention of Subway, who quickly put him in a regional, Midwest TV commercial. Before long, Fogle was starring in a national campaign as America's latest fitness hero.

He's gone on to the college lecture circuit, guested on *Oprah Winfrey* and *Larry King Live*, written a book about his adventures (*Jared, the Subway Guy: Winning through Losing: 13 Lessons for Turning Your Life Around*), and teamed with WWE wrestler John Cena for a series of comical Subway ads in 2006.

Almost immediately, rumors that Fogle had died began to circulate on the Web. It was as if losing weight through fast food was just too much for some folks to digest. Unattributed reports suggested Fogle had been arrested for cocaine possession and was immediately dropped by Subway as a spokesperson. Another suggested the truth behind his dramatic weight loss was that he had a gastric bypass operation. Still another said his weight loss could be attributed to the fact he had AIDS.

These vicious attacks could stem from any number of reasons. People have become so bored and jaded with instant celebrities—everyone from *Survivor* or *Amazing Race* contestants to skinny Subway sandwich eaters—that they can hardly wait to tear them down as fast as they build them up. Viewers who have been duped into believing diet and exercise was behind a TV star's weight loss—only to see tabloid headlines about secret bypass surgery—are cynical about any diet hype. (Former *View* cohost Star Jones went through similar scrutiny before finally admitting that bypass surgery helped her shed 160 pounds.) Or maybe a few million overstuffed McDonald's or Kentucky Fried Chicken (KFC) patrons simply resented Subway Boy's sudden fame and fortune.

In any event, the producers of *South Park* certainly did Fogle no favors when they released a 2002 episode titled, "Jared Has Aides." In the episode, Fogle comes to South Park, where he's a hero to Cartman and the kids. He decides to come clean on his real diet secret: he has AIDS.

Actually, he has aides, trainers, people who help him lose weight. It just sounds like he's saying he has AIDS. "I want everyone here to get AIDS," the cartoon Fogle says. "I am even going to help children in underprivileged countries get AIDS." The townspeople react in horror, as did many viewers.

"What a sad reflection of society today," said Rick Hollingsworth, a Canadian AIDS activist who contacted the *Toronto Sun* about the episode. The producers defended their animated antics as simply more envelope pushing. "We wanted to put it on the table," said *South Park* cocreator Matt Stone. "People always said you can't do jokes about AIDS. We say maybe you can if you do it in a stupid way like this."

Stone also invoked Woody Allen's mantra: "Comedy is tragedy plus time." He cited an example from a recent magazine article—enslavement of Hebrews, funny; enslavement of blacks, not funny.

But AIDS? Funny? Hollingsworth could barely speak. "Try explaining that," he said, "to five million AIDS orphans around the world." For his part, Fogle seemed to take the *South Park* ribbing in stride. In a 2003 *Washington Post* interview, he said, "You know you've made it when shows like *South Park* start parodying you."

RUMOR: *The original network run of* The Flintstones *was sponsored by a cigarette company.*

TRUE: *Yabba dabba don't. As in smoke, kids. But that's just what cartoon caveman Fred Flintstone did in ads that accompanied the original ABC prime time run of the series.*

The Flintstones ran from 1960 to 1966. Back then, cigarette advertising was a big part of the TV landscape. America's favorite TV couple from the

'50s, Lucille Ball and Desi Arnaz, were often seem extolling the virtues of Phillip Morris cigarettes between station breaks on *I Love Lucy*. Dick Van Dyke and Mary Tyler Moore can occasionally be spotted puffing on Kent cigarettes on reruns of *The Dick Van Dyke Show*. Even *The Addams Family* was "brought to you by Dutch Masters cigars."

These shows were part of an era when a primary sponsor literally bankrolled an entire series. The first two seasons of *The Flintstones* were partially sponsored by R. J. Reynolds, makers of Winston cigarettes. In one unbelievable (by today's standards) spot, Fred and Barney are seen having a smoke in the backyard, while their wives, Wilma and Betty, do all the yard work. In another, Fred lights one up for Wilma, invoking the sponsor's slogan, "Winston tastes good like a cigarette should."

RUMOR: *The actor who portrayed the "Marlboro Man" in print and television cigarette advertisements died of lung cancer.*

TRUE: *And not once, but twice. The headlines spelled it out in 1992: "Marlboro Man Killed by Lung Cancer" (The Daily Telegraph). "A Rough Ride" (The New York Times). "Lung Cancer Ends Life of Former Marlboro Man" (Los Angeles Times). They were from stories reporting the death of Wayne McLaren, a one-time professional rodeo rider who modeled for a Marlboro Man cigarette print campaign in 1976. After a pack and a half a day smoking habit, he succumbed to cancer at 51.*

In one of his last interviews, for the Associated Press, McLaren admitted his 25-year smoking habit had caught up with him. "I've spent the last month of my life in an incubator and I'm telling you," he said, "it's not worth it."

Later, in 1995, another actor, David McLean, died after being diagnosed with lung cancer; he was 73. McLean's Marlboro Man credentials were even stronger, appearing in several TV and print campaigns dating back to the early '60s.

McLaren and McLean were not the only men to don the Stetson and ride through Marlboro country. Oklahoma native Darrell Winfield smoked his way through several print campaigns in the mid-70s. Former New York Giants quarterback Charley Conerly also wore the Marlboro Stetson.

But, several wrongful death court cases later, the company that made Marlboro cigarettes, Phillip Morris, eventually acknowledged that both McLaren and McLean had belonged to their Marlboro ranch. The irony that these rugged cowboys were killed not by silver bullets but by the very thing they were promoting was not lost on proponents of the antismoking movement.

Just before his death, McLaren took part in a moving spot that juxtaposed his handsome cowboy cigarette ad image with a shot of him wasting away in a hospital bed. One antismoking print ad, designed in the familiar outdoorsy Marlboro style, showed two cowboys on horseback having a man to man moment. The caption: "Bob, I've got emphysema."

In 2006, *USA Today* ranked the Marlboro Man as number 1 on their list of the 101 most influential people who never lived. He ~~never~~ even lives on in film: a fictional variation of the Marlboro Man appears in the satirical feature *Thank You for Smoking* (2006). Sam Elliott plays a dying former Marlboro Man bought off by a tobacco lobbyist. Put that in your pipe and smoke it.

RUMOR: You can see part of a skydiver's last, fatal dive in a Mountain Dew commercial.

FALSE: Although this one was based on a true tragic incident. On December 14, 1995—a day shy of his 29th birthday—world champion sky surfer Rob Harris was shooting a daring stunt scene in the skies over British Columbia for a Mountain Dew ad. The James Bond spoof had Harris, dressed in a tuxedo, leaping from an exploding plane. Somehow, Harris's chute got tangled, and by the time he opened his reserve, it was too late—he fell to his death.

The rumor, spread on the Internet through a series of e-mails, suggested that portions of Harris's fatal jump actually wound up in the finished soda spot. Here's some text from one of the Internet hoaxes, dated 1996, as posted on Snopes.com:

> Apparently his parents believe that he would have wanted the commercial to air so his friends could see it, so Mountain Dew finished the ad, but next time you are watching, know that in a mere few seconds after the parachute is released, that guy is dead.

Subsequent postings cite the ad as a commercial for 7UP; using footage from the fatal jump is justified because "it is so good."

The thing is, Rob Harris did die, he died shooting a Mountain Dew ad, and the Mountain Dew ad aired with footage of Harris shot earlier that same day. As the headline in *People* magazine read, "Behind a Zany Mountain Dew Ad Lies the Sad Saga of the Death of Pro Skydiver Rob Harris" (July 15, 1996). The *People* article goes on to explain that Harris's parents were approached by Pepsico, which owns Mountain Dew, and asked if a scene from one of Harris's earlier jumps could be included in the final ad.

Somewhat reluctantly, they gave their okay. "Rob would have wanted it, and his friends really looked forward to seeing it, and so do we," they were quoted as saying. Confusion in regard to this rumor is easy to understand. Even the *New York Times* erroneously reported that footage of Harris's final jump wound up in the finished ad.

One footnote: musician Alan Parson's 1996 song "Free Fall," heard on his *On Air* album, is dedicated to Harris's memory.

RUMOR: Taco Bell stopped using that little dog in its ad campaigns because the owner had him put to sleep.

FALSE: The big-eyed Chihuahua behind that famous phrase—"Yo quiero Taco Bell"—was introduced to America in 1997. Gidget was the actual name of the spunky little canine used in the TV ads. She was voiced by Carlos Alazaqui (the voice of Rocko from the animated kiddie show Rocko's Modern Life*).*

Contrary to legend, Gidget didn't get booted out of Taco Bell's campaigns because she was squashed by a studio light or frozen to death in the cargo hold of a commercial airliner. Another rumor suggested the pooch was killed so that Taco Bell wouldn't have to pay the full value of the dog's contract.

Again, as cited on Snopes.com (and identified as an Internet rumor that circulated in 2003):

> A friend was telling me he had heard that Taco Bell had the Chihuahua dog it used in its advertising put to sleep, rather than honoring the full length of the contract with the animal's owner.

And earlier, from 1998:

> I've been hearing a rumble for the last couple of days about the dog in the Taco Bell commercials. Seems the little bastard got loose during a break in filming, ran into the path of a dollying film camera, and was crushed, yea unto death.

As Bart Simpson used to say, "Ay carumba." The doggie death rumors started after Taco Bell abruptly yanked the pooch out of their promotions in 2000. The reason? Simple, really. Sales were down and the mutt wasn't moving any burritos. Taco Bell decided to go in a different direction.

This just didn't make sense to TV viewers who looked forward to the often funny and memorable spots. The Taco Bell dog had become a staple of the late night talk show circuit and even inspired a ditty by Adam Sandler ("I Ran over the Taco Bell Dog"). Taco Bell customers reportedly bought 13 million Chihuahua plush toys.

It didn't make sense to the ad agency executive who was axed in 2000 along with Gidget. "People like the dog," TBWA/Chiat Day chief executive Tom Carroll told the Associated Press. "It's just that simple."

That's why this rumor continues to dog Taco Bell—yo quiero little Gidget. Suggesting the campaign ended because the dog died overlooks one important fact: there are billions of other Chihuahuas out there. Just as there was never just one Lassie, there could have been a dozen Taco Bell dogs.

As for Gidget, she had a thriving career years after her gig ended as a fast food fido. She can be spotted as Bruiser's mom in the 2003 Reese Witherspoon feature *Legally Blonde 2: Red, White, and Blonde*.

RUMOR: "Crying Indian" Iron Eyes Cody from those famous antipollution spots from the '70s wasn't really a Native American but was of Italian descent.

TRUE: Fans of The Sopranos *may recall that the Italian American outing of this environmental ad icon was a comical subplot to one third-season episode of the mob drama.*

The original, minute-long ad premiered way back in 1971. It showed what looked like a Native American paddling past erupting smokestacks through a filthy, polluted river. A passing motorist carelessly tosses trash out his window, landing right at the Indian's feet. The camera zooms in to his face, revealing a single tear rolling down his cheek. The voice-over states, "People start pollution; people can stop it."

While Cody often claimed to be of Cherokee/Cree extraction, his parents were both Italian immigrants. Born in 1904, his real name was Espera DeCorti. He shortened that to Cody after moving to Hollywood in the '20s, where he found work in dozens of movies and TV shows, including *Bonanza*, *Gunsmoke*, and *Rawhide*. He appeared with the likes of Roy Rogers and later Richard Harris (in *A Man Called Horse*).

Here's where it gets interesting. Cody may not have been a full-blood Indian, but he lived his life as one, marrying a Native American woman and adopting two Indian boys. He was seldom seen without his beaded moccasins or buckskin jacket. He sported a braided wig on his head. His long-standing work on behalf of Native American culture was recognized in 1995 when Hollywood's Native American community honored him for all his charitable deeds. He died in 1999 at the age of 94.

CHAPTER 8

Would You Believe...?
Strange Stories from the '60s

s his TV alter ego, Maxwell Smart, aka Agent 86, Don Adams got to utter a lot of memorable catchphrases. "Sorry about that, chief," "Missed it by that much," and, "Would you believe..." were three sayings Adams made famous during the run of the '60s' spy spoof *Get Smart*.

"Would you believe..." could also apply to several TV legends, myths, and rumors of the '60s, a decade that seemed to be particularly rich in rumors. Maybe there was something in the air, or something people were smoking, or just a great time to make stuff up before the advent of the Internet. Whatever the reason, here are some tall TV tales from the '60s.

RUMOR: Jim Nabors married Rock Hudson.

FALSE: As Gomer Pyle would say, "Surprise, surprise, surprise!" This rumor really isn't true, but, much to their dismay, it stuck to these two like glue. Back when he was still in the closet, Hudson simply snapped, "No comment," when asked about it by People *magazine.*

The rumor surfaced around 1970, at a time when homosexuality was a career killer in Hollywood and same sex unions were as unknown and as unreachable as life on Mars. Jim Nabors's service sitcom, *Gomer Pyle U.S.M.C.*, was a top-10 hit for five consecutive years in the '60s on CBS. The genial Alabama native had played the country bumpkin character previously on the equally popular *Andy Griffith Show*. So while he always played a naive second banana, Nabors was as popular as any star on television throughout that decade.

Hudson had established himself as a romantic leading man with a light touch for comedy through a string of hit films in the late '50s and '60s, including *Giant* and *Pillow Talk*. He would later enjoy success in television opposite Susan Saint James in the "he and she" police drama *McMillan and Wife* (1971–77).

In 1970, the idea that the two had been married would have been shocking first and funny second. Few people back then would have accepted that these two popular stars were both closeted homosexuals, let alone married to each other.

The source of the rumor was apparently a wedding invitation that was sent out as a practical joke. Hudson, who coauthored (with Sara Davidson) the bestselling biography *Rock Hudson: His Story*, claimed the source of the rumor was "a couple of elderly or middle-aged homosexuals who live in Huntington Beach" who threw a huge party every year, inviting everyone they knew—as many as 500 people. Each year they sent out an engraved invitation with an outlandish theme. One year it would read something like, "You are cordially invited to the coronation of Queen Elizabeth in Huntington Beach." The year in question, however, the invitation read, "You are cordially invited to the wedding reception of Rock Hudson and Jim Nabors."

As Hudson recalls, the rumor "went all over the country." Keep in mind, this crazy bit of gossip spread years before the Internet and e-mail were a factor. Jokes about the Nabors/Hudson wedding were reaching school yards as far away as Canada. In a 1998 *TV Guide* article, author Davidson said she "could never find a shred" of evidence that Nabors and Hudson ever had a relationship, although they did know each other and had, on at least one occasion, guest starred together on *The Carol Burnett Show*. (They were also once photographed together at a Burnett Caesars Palace opening in 1970).

The missing "smoking gun" in all of this is the mock wedding invitation. You'd think one lucky recipient would have held onto it after all these years or sold it either to the *National Enquirer* or on eBay. But Google it all you want, it never turns up.

Hudson's shocking 1986 death from complications of AIDS only revived the old Nabors wedding rumors. The movie star's illness forced him to come out and admit his sexual orientation.

Nabors has never discussed his private life. He had successful liver transplant surgery in 1994 and lives in Hawaii, where he grows macadamia nuts.

To add insult to injury, National Lampoon once announced, in a parody of *Newsweek*'s "passages" section, that Hudson and Nabors had gotten a divorce. Shey-zam!

RUMOR: Holy wardrobe malfunction! Back when he was playing Robin in Batman, *Burt Ward's tights exposed a little too much—so he was forced to take a pill to help hide his "Bat pole."*

TRUE: *Ward told all in his salacious 1995 autobiography* Boy Wonder: My Life in Tights. *It seems those tights were a bit too tight for the Catholic Legion of Decency, especially back when* Batman *premiered early in 1966. They complained to ABC that Ward's costume was too revealing for the innocent Bat-fans watching at home.*

"Oh, God, the python pants. They were horrible," Ward told TV critics at a 2003 CBS press event to promote the reunion movie *Return to the Batcave: The Misadventures of Adam and Burt.*

At first, when he was told to take a pill that would reduce his, uh, part, Ward thought the producers were joking. It was no joke, however. "I almost lost my job over this," said Ward, who to this day doesn't know exactly what kind of pill he ended up taking. Just 20 years old and a complete newcomer to the acting business at the time *Batman* launched, Ward swallowed his pride and swallowed the pill. "It was pretty upsetting to me," he said, "because the concept was, if this really works so well, maybe it's going to have a lasting effect."

Clearly, as Ward recounts in way too much detail in his book, there were no lasting side effects. *My Life in Tights* is filled with stories about his many romantic conquests during and after the series. "Actually, I held back a lot of stories," he said at CBS's after party in 2003. Adam West, who played Batman, was no altar boy either, according to Ward. "There were any number of cities we were asked to leave."

Batman, which aired twice a week for most of its three season run, was an instant hit with kids. The superhero series had a hefty $800,000 a week budget and no bump was going to bump it off ABC's schedule. "*Batman* was so successful you had psychiatrists analyzing these relationships and you had all these people getting into the act," said Ward.

Born Bert John Gervis in 1945, Ward is now a roly-poly Robin who looks more like The Penguin. He was working for a real estate company when he decided to audition for the role of Batman's young crime-fighting protégé. At the time he had never even read a Batman comic. His "Holy amateur night!" delivery was exactly what the producers were looking for to help camp up the series.

Still, he almost lost his job for a reason that had nothing to do with his shorts. He kept getting injured doing his own stunts during the pilot, including one explosives misfire that resulted in a third degree burn to his arm. "Four of the first five days of shooting, I was in the hospital," said Ward. "I didn't think I was going to survive the first episode. Fortunately, as the Legion of Decency noted, he was able to stick it out.

Ward addressed one other Bat-rumor: that Frank Sinatra wanted to play The Joker. The series attracted several big name guest stars during its run, including Burgess Meredith (as The Penguin), Frank Gorshin (The Riddler), Julie Newmar (Catwoman), and Vincent Price (Egghead). Milton Berle, Liberace, Eartha Kitt, Joan Collins, Shelley Winters, and Tallulah Bankhead all got into the act.

Although he refused to shave his moustache (it was hidden under lots of white clown makeup), Hollywood veteran Cesar Romero captured the role of The Joker. "From what I understand, Frank Sinatra was very upset because he couldn't play The Joker," said Ward. "Cesar Romero had already been signed." Sinatra's Rat Pack pal Sammy Davis, Jr., did make a *Batman* appearance, popping his head out of a window during one of the cheesy scenes where the Dynamic Duo scale a wall.

West, forever Batman to boomers who grew up with the series, recalled another unlikely celebrity who wanted to make a cameo: Robert Kennedy. Then attorney general, he apparently lobbied to make a window-popping appearance. He didn't get that (although former JFK presidential press secretary Pierre Salinger did, guesting as Lucky Pierre after bumping into *Batman* producer Bill Dozier at a cocktail party), but he did get an autographed photo of West, which Kennedy hung in his office. "I signed it," deadpanned West, "'From one crime fighter to another.'"

RUMOR: Dick York, the actor who played the original Darren on Bewitched, *was fired from the series by producer William Asher after getting too cozy with Asher's wife, series star Elizabeth Montgomery.*

FALSE: It is a credit to both York and Montgomery that they both looked so married and affectionate on Bewitched *that some people assumed the reason York was no longer on the show was that he had fallen under the star's spell. The series, about a suburban witch and her uptight advertising executive husband—who just happened to be a mortal—was ABC's biggest hit of the '60s.*

York, a veteran of stage and screen, was cast as Darren Stevens when the show was launched in 1964. He and Montgomery had instant chemistry, and the show became a hit. Unfortunately, York had damaged his back several years earlier while working on the long-forgotten movie *They Came to Cordura* (1959), which costarred Gary Cooper, Rita Hayworth, and Van Heflin. On the second to last day on the set of the Spanish Civil War picture, York was propelling a hand car with Cooper along a railway track when a cast member accidentally grabbed one of the handles, forcing York to lift about 180 pounds more weight than he expected. As a result, he tore the muscles along the right side of his back. His spine healed incorrectly and he spent the rest of his life in pain.

The bad back bothered him a year later while shooting *Inherit the Wind* with Spencer Tracy and had become almost unbearable by the time he won the part on *Bewitched*. There were days when he would get shots of cortisone and novocaine into his back just to get through a scene.

In his autobiography, *Seasaw Girl*, York recounts how he had to be lifted down from a scaffolding during a setup for a special effects shot. He literally passed out on the way down and woke to horrified stares from his costars. He apparently had had some sort of fit from all the medication he was taking just to try and stay on the job.

York was in the hospital when Asher came to visit and asked him if he wanted to quit the series. As York recounts in his book, he replied, "If it's all right with you, Billy." Asher knew York had had enough. The actor remained sick and on his back for over a year.

The series went on without him. After several episodes aired with Darren "out of town," a new Darren, played by actor Dick Sargent, took over the role in 1969. While *Bewitched* stayed on the air another three seasons, it was never the same. The supernatural sitcom instantly dropped 13 places in the ratings.

"I knew it was inevitable that he would have to be replaced," remembers Erin Murphy, who, together with twin sister Diane, played the Stevens' bewitching daughter Tabitha on the series. Even though she was only five or six at the time, Murphy could tell that York "was sick for almost an entire season. I saw that he was in a lot of pain and often had to sit down or lay against the set."

Asher, who attended a 2005 TV critics press conference honoring several broadcasting legends, said it was hard to watch York struggle through his scenes. "We were aware of it for a couple of years and it kept getting worse and worse," said Asher. "Very sad." He said he never heard the rumors that York had been fired for getting too kissy-face with his wife, Montgomery. (The two separated shortly after *Bewitched* left the air in 1972.)

After years of chronic back pain and emphysema, York passed away on February 20, 1992.

RUMOR: The night the Beatles made their North American debut on The Ed Sullivan Show *in February of 1964, no major crimes were reported in New York City.*

UNSUBSTANTIATED: It certainly seemed like the world came to a halt on February 9, 1964, when The Beatles took America by storm on The Ed Sullivan Show. *The TV audience that night was massive. More than 70 million viewers tuned in, ranking it as one of the most-watched TV shows ever. But were a disproportionate number of New York City burglars big Beatles fans?*

In Hunter Davies's authorized biography of The Beatles, first published in 1968, he writes the following of the Fab Four's first *Ed Sullivan Show* appearance: "In New York, during the show, not one hubcap from a car was stolen. Throughout America, so it was reported, not one major crime was committed by a teenager."

Even George Harrison, in *The Beatles Anthology*, remarked that he heard there were "no reported crimes, or very few, when The Beatles were on *The Ed Sullivan Show*, even the criminals had a rest for 10 minutes."

While it is possible that The Beatles so consumed interest at all levels on that night, it is very hard to trace actual crime statistics for the hour they were on the show. It should also be noted that while the 73 million people who tuned in represented about 40 percent of the U.S. viewing audience at that time, another 60 percent were free to loot, steal, and plunder.

RUMOR: Ed Sullivan once introduced Shelley Winters as Shelley Berman.

TRUE: Radio wit Fred Allen once said, "Ed Sullivan will be around as long as someone else has talent." Jack Benny once asked Ed Sullivan what exactly he did on his long-running CBS variety hour, The Ed Sullivan Show *(1948–71). Sullivan replied, "I introduce the acts."*

Even that he didn't do particularly well. Sullivan routinely slouched, hunched, fumbled, and forgot. Pure showmanship got him through 23 seasons of jugglers, plate spinners, singers, comedians, puppeteers, and ventriloquists.

Among his actual, on-air gaffes are these beauties: "Now let's hear it really big for singer Jose Feliciano. He's blind...and he's Puerto Rican!" He once introduced Sergio Franci as "Sergio Finko...I mean Sergio Freako...I mean Fergio Stinko."

On the other hand, Sullivan never said: "Here's a production note: *The Invisible Man* will not be seen tonight." Various Sullivan imitators (and there were many, including Will Jordan (*Down with Love*), made up lines that have come to be attributed to the wooden TV host. None was ever as funny as Sullivan's own goofy gaffes.

RUMOR: There was no "small step" by a man on the moon in 1969, as the Apollo missions were all faked in a TV studio.

FALSE: Poll after poll continues to show that a significant portion of the U.S. population still believes that the moon missions and landings of the late-60s/early '70s were faked. According to a 1999 Gallup poll, 6 percent of the American public believes the initial landing was a hoax (another 89% believed they it did occur, while a few had no opinion).

A Fox TV special about conspiracy theories stirred this one up again in 2001. There was also a whole movie made about it, sort of—1978's *Capricorn One.* James Brolin, Sam Waterston, and O.J. Simpson starred as three astronauts who, at the last second and at the urging of the government, bail out of a mission to Mars. They later agree to take part in a cover-up which eventually puts their lives at risk. The movie's tag line: "The mission was a sham. The murders were real."

That movie was shot in California. The moon landing footage was, according to conspiracy theorists, shot somewhere in the Nevada desert or in a TV studio, not on the surface of the moon.

Now, we love rumors and conspiracy theories as much as the next guy, enough in fact to write a whole book about them. But, please, next you'll be telling me Jerry Lewis is a hero in France.

CHAPTER 9

That '70s Show: Growing up with *The Brady Bunch* and *The Partridge Family*

Movie stars, pop icons, Star Fleet commanders, superheroes—no one was immune from rumors or urban legends in the '60s and '70s, and the crazier the better.

In their 1984 book *Rumor!* Hal Morgan and Kerry Tucker theorize that it is "insideness" that compels people to invent, repeat, and spread wild rumors about famous people and institutions. Especially in this age of instant Internet access and constant tabloid TV scrutiny, people always want to seem to be in the know, to have the inside scoop.

Yet some of the craziest rumors emerged in the '60s and '70s, years before computers became an important part of virtually every home. Proving that you don't need a computer, just word of mouth, to spread a tall tale across a continent, here are a couple of gems from the '70s from two of the most popular musical family sitcoms of the day. Both involve rumors of romantic relationships between costars. One is true, one of false, and both are, as Marsha Brady might have said, "Gross."

RUMOR: *David Cassidy, who played heartthrob Danny Partridge on the early '70s' comedy* The Partridge Family, *dated the actress who played his sister, Susan Dey.*

TRUE: *Cassidy admitted the liaison at a 2004 TV critics press tour session in Los Angeles. "After the show ended, we dated a couple of times," he said. "I loved her like a sister." "Well, that's gross," said Danny Bonaduce, who was sitting next to him at the press conference.*

Bonaduce played Cassidy's freckle-faced kid brother Danny. Loosely based on the actual family band The Cowsills, *The Partridge Family* (1970–74) starred Shirley Jones as a widowed mom who toured the country in a multi-colored school bus with her five pop star children.

Both Cassidy (*C'mon Get Happy: Fear and Loathing on the Partridge Family Bus*) and Bonaduce (*Random Acts of Badness*) have released tell-all autobiographies. Among the stories they've spilled is one about Dey's odd eating disorder during production of the series. "One year Susan Dey stopped eating anything but carrots," said Bonaduce. "The woman turned orange."

Bonaduce also cleared up another urban legend that clings to his '70s sitcom: that Jeremy Gelbwaks—the child actor who played pint-sized drummer Christopher in the first season of *The Partridge Family*—grew up to become Axl Rose. Not true, says Bonaduce, who nevertheless lost all contact with Gelbwaks. "Who the hell knows whatever became of that guy?"

Actually, Danny, Gelbwaks—who was nine when the series launched— left *The Partridge Family* after one season because his family moved to Virginia. He worked in the computer industry before becoming a management consultant. Talk about not becoming your brother's keeper.

RUMOR: *Barry Williams, who played oldest son Greg Brady on* The Brady Bunch, *had a sexual relationship offscreen with the actress who played his mother on the series, Florence Henderson.*

FALSE: *Marsha, Marsha, Marsha! Why was your older brother Greg boasting about dating his mom on* The Brady Bunch?

The Brady Bunch, a show so uncool it took 30 years of constant reruns to become cool, ran on ABC between 1969 and 1974. It was the brainchild of Sherwood Schwartz, a TV producer often lambasted as the daddy of schlock TV, with *Gilligan's Island* among his other cornball credits.

Still, there is—among boomers, at least—a great deal of lingering affection for *The Brady Bunch*. Daytime talk show host Kelly Ripa, who hosted the 2007 TV Land Awards (where *The Brady Bunch* was saluted) told me she grew up with dreams of someday moving into the Brady house. "I thought I was a Brady," said Ripa, who grew up in New Jersey. "I wanted to live in that beautiful, contemporary house in California, with all those earth tones and that orange Formica kitchen. We had an orange Formica kitchen, too."

The idea that there was any hanky panky going on behind the scenes of this ridiculously wholesome family sitcom made all the rumors that much more irresistible, especially to boomers who grew up with the series. That was something oldest Brady son Barry Williams seemed ready and eager to capitalize on in his 1992 bestseller, *"Growing up Brady: I Was a Teenage Greg."*

Among his more titillating revelations: he dated costar Maureen McCormick, who played eldest daughter Marsha Brady "off and on from year three through year five." Williams said he had the hots for McCormick pretty much from the first casting sessions on. "I knew I was going to have to be patient because she was only 12," he said. "Fortunately, our series lasted a long five years and patience paid off." Creepy.

Williams also spilled the beans that youngest TV siblings Bobby (Michael Lookingland) and Cindy (Susan Olsen) were once caught making out in the Brady's backyard doghouse. Woof!

The Williams/Henderson hook up story probably sold more books than any other Brady rumor. Henderson was 20 years Williams's senior, turning 40 the year the series went off the air. Williams says he had a crush on his TV mom and finally worked up the nerve to ask her out to dinner once the series wrapped. Henderson was married at the time with four children of her own (she used to fly home to New York from Los Angeles, where *The Brady Bunch* was filmed, every weekend). She accepted Williams's dinner invitation, but to hear her tell it, the whole thing has been blown way out of proportion.

"I guess in a sense it was a date," she writes on her Web site, "Because Barry thought it was. But of course, I had no idea that his intentions were to 'date' me. It has made for a good story, though!"

Both Williams and Henderson continue to appear at various *Brady Bunch* reunions and tributes. Both have also been roughed up in reality television, with Williams stooping to brawl with former *Partridge Family* bad boy Danny Bonaduce in FOX's überexploitative *Celebrity Boxing* (which Bonaduce won easily). Henderson appeared on one of the editions of VH1's *The Surreal Life*, also not a career high point.

Christopher Knight, who played middle Brady son Peter, also appeared on *The Surreal Life*, where he met *America's Next Top Model* winner Adrianne Curry. The two eventually got married and starred in their own spin-off reality series, *My Fair Brady*.

At a press tour session for that series, Knight was asked if he even snuck a little smooch with TV mom Henderson. "No, that was Barry's playground," was his gallant reply.

CHAPTER 10

Monkee Business: Are You a Believer? Check out These Monkee Myths

Since, as Fred Allen once said, "imitation is the sincerest form of television," it was only a matter of time before some smart producer and network tapped into the enormous international success of The Beatles. And so began *The Monkees,* a sitcom about four Beatle look-alikes whose weekly adventures were largely inspired by the fun and music found in *A Hard Day's Night* and *Help!*

The series starred Micky Dolenz, Davy Jones, Michael Nesmith, and Peter Tork, chosen as much for their look and acting chops as their ability to handle guitars and vocals.

In his 1993 autobiography, *I'm a Believer: My Life of Monkees, Music, and Madness,* Dolenz takes issue with the idea that The Monkees were America's answer to The Beatles. "That would be like saying *Star Trek* was Hollywood's answer to NASA's space program," he wrote. Dolenz had to agree with, of all people, John Lennon, who once remarked that The Monkees reminded him of The Marx Brothers. "The Monkees were The Marx Brothers with long hair," agreed Dolenz.

While the series only lasted two seasons, the group scored several number one hits and has enjoyed a surprisingly enduring popularity, especially when reruns found a new home on MTV in the mid-80s. A sold out reunion concert tour in 1986—20 years after their series premiered—ranked them as the number one musical touring attraction that year.

The success of The Monkees also demonstrated the power of television to establish pop idols, a lesson not lost on the producers of the biggest TV hit so far of this century—*American Idol*. Other popular groups borne more out of marketing than musical ability, from The Spice Girls to The Pussycat Dolls, have followed in The Monkees's pre-fab footprints.

They've also inspired a couple of pretty wild rumors and popular myths. That most turn out to be true is enough to make daydream believers out of all of us.

RUMOR: Hundreds auditioned for the '60s' series The Monkees. *One of them was future serial killer Charles Manson.*

FALSE: "Untrue. Urban myth, I'm afraid," says Micky Dolenz, who together with Jones, Nesmith, and Tork, aced the auditions and became the "Pre-Fab Four."

In September of 1965, they all answered the following ad that appeared in *Daily Variety*: "4 Insane Boys, Age 17–21" sought for "Acting Roles in New TV Series." The idea was to spin a TV show off of the fun and free-spirited Beatle movies *A Hard Day's Night* and *Help!*

Four hundred and thirty-seven Monkee wannabes applied, but, according to Dolenz, not one of them was Charles Manson. While he might have qualified as "insane," Manson was already well past the age range posted by the producers. That September, he was 31.

He was also behind bars. Among other crimes, Manson was indicted for violating the Mann Act in 1960 and was incarcerated at the U.S. penitentiary at McNeil Island in Washington in 1961. After five years there, he was transferred to Terminal Island, San Pedro, California, where he was released on March 21, 1967.

Still, the rumor persists to this day, occasionally popping up in print, that he was at the audition. Maybe it's because there seems to be six degrees of separation between The Monkees and so many other headline makers of the '60s. For example: Jack Nicholson cowrote their trippy 1968 feature *Head*—true. Glen Campbell used to play and sing on Monkee records—true. Davy Jones (in the cast of *Oliver!* at the time) shared the stage of *The Ed Sullivan Show* the night The Beatles conquered America—true.

It's also true that future rockers Stephen Stills, Three Dog Night's Danny Hutton, and Paul Williams were all at that Monkees audition, as was former Mouseketeer and *Donna Reed Show* child star Paul Petersen. Throwing Manson's name into the mix just adds a lurid charge to the legend.

Another auditioner, longtime Los Angeles DJ Rodney Bingenheimer (profiled in the 2005 documentary *Mayor of the Sunset Strip*), has always maintained that Manson was also at the casting call. Manson did later hang with Byrds' producer Terry Melcher (it was at his former house in Hollywood where the Sharon Tate murders took place) and lived for a while with Beach Boy drummer Dennis Wilson. One Manson composition—"Never Learn Not to Love"—even wound up as the B-side of a Beach Boys single. In 1968, they performed it on, of all places, *The Mike Douglas Show*.

Forty years later, Dolenz is not a believer of this persistent Monkees myth, although he was in no real position to confirm or deny it. Dolenz was never at that original Monkees cattle call audition and never even saw the ad calling for "4 insane boys." With a track record as an established actor (he had been a child star of the late-50s' adventure series *Circus Boy*), his agent simply arranged for Dolenz to make a private audition.

Interviewed in 2006 during rehearsals in Toronto for a theatrical revival of *Pippin*, the then 61-year-old actor/singer said it's something he's discussed with *Monkees'* producers Bob Rafelson and Bert Schneider. "You never know, he could have shown up at some cattle call, early audition and met with some casting people. But no one remembers," says Dolenz.

The other reason the rumor persists is that the one guy who could confirm or deny it has never addressed it. A request to interview Manson, now in his 70s and serving a life sentence in California's Corcoran State Prison, was denied.

RUMOR: *Michael Nesmith didn't need his Monkee money—he got rich because his mother invented Liquid Paper.*

TRUE: *This Monkees mom learned from her mistakes. Bette Nesmith Graham, a Corpus Christi, Texas native, gave birth to Michael in 1942. Her husband Warren went off to fight in World War II. While he survived the war and returned to Texas, they were divorced in 1946.*

In order to earn a living to support herself and her son, young Bette worked at a bank. Her typing skills helped her become an executive secretary. She picked up extra money decorating the bank windows with holiday themes.

Correcting mistakes on those early electric typewriters was painstaking and time consuming. When she was hand lettering copy as a window artist, she observed that mistakes were rarely corrected. They were simply painted over. Why not apply that fix to typing?

Nesmith Graham concocted a mixture of white tempera water-based paint in a bottle which she took to the office. Using a small paint brush, she started dabbing out her typing mistakes with paint and typing over them.

She perfected her paint and type technique for about five years. When she noticed coworkers clamoring for some of her mistake paint, she decided that there was probably a market for her invention.

In 1956, she began marketing her miracle correction liquid as Mistake Out, later changing the name to Liquid Paper when she started her own company.

In a 1999 *TV Guide* article, Michael Nesmith was quick to point out that he wasn't just slumming it as a pretend rock star on a TV show while waiting to inherit his mother's Liquid Paper fortune. Nesmith insisted that "Liquid Paper did not get big until the late '70s." By then, Nesmith had already been through the rise and fall of Monkee mania.

The series ran on NBC from 1966 to 1968, with Nesmith and the other three members of the so-called "Pre-Fab Four" selling millions of records (including the top-selling American release of 1967, "I'm a Believer") before attempting to take their act on the road as a real pop band. Creative tensions within the group, however, along with the cancellation of their TV show, led to a split. The group disbanded in 1970.

So the idea that Nesmith was some rich kid goofing off as a pretend rock star, waiting to inherit his mother's fortune, is not exactly true. Still, in 1979, after offering it first to IBM, Bette Nesmith Graham sold Liquid Paper to Gillette for $47.5 million plus a royalty on every bottle sold until the year 2000.

Upon her death the very next year, Michael Nesmith inherited half her estate. The other half went to the Gihon Foundation, a group, according to its Web site, dedicated to the "pursuit of entrepreneurial philanthropy." Once a year, "thought leaders from different disciplines" debate the most important issues of the day. Nesmith heads the group's four-member board of trustees.

Which answers the musical question: how do you go from Monkee to trustee? Take the last train to Clarksville. Pass the Liquid Paper.

RUMOR: Jimi Hendrix was once the opening act for The Monkees.

TRUE: Okay, so this was never a rumor or legend, just a fact. But, hey, c'mon, it sounds like somebody made it up.

In 1967, the four individuals who starred in *The Monkees* TV show were trying to prove to the world they really could be a band by going on the road and touring. This wasn't a big problem for Nesmith and Tork, already accomplished guitarists. Dolenz and Jones, however, were actors first, singers second. Dolenz was "cast" as The Monkees' drummer simply because Jones, at five foot three, disappeared behind the drum kit. Suddenly, Dolenz, who had never picked up a drumstick before *The Monkees*, was thrust into concerts where he had to keep up with professional musicians.

That he and the others more or less pulled it off is commendable. Certainly most of the young, screaming fans didn't care if Micky was banging out of time. But booking the world's greatest rock guitarist as your opening act is laughable. If The Monkees were looking for a sure way to alienate both critics and their fans, this was it. Whose dumb idea was this?

Turns out it was Micky Dolenz's. He was a big fan of The Jimi Hendrix Experience, having caught the trio in New York and at the Monterey pop music festival where their electric performance stole the show. Dolenz figured Hendrix's theatrical flair (he used to play the guitar with his teeth and famously set fire to it at Monterey) was perfect for The Monkees and suggested The Experience—still more famous in England than America—as a perfect opening act for their summer tour. The concert promoters, including Dick Clark, agreed and The Experience were booked.

"Unfortunately," wrote Dolenz, "it did become rather awkward. Jimi would amble out onto the stage, fire up the amps, and break into 'Purple Haze,' and the kids in the audience instantly drown him out with, 'We want Daaavy!' God, it was embarrassing."

Hendrix suffered through seven humiliating shows and then quit the tour. The only reason he and his comanager, Chas Chandler, agreed to the gig in the first place, was to try and get the most possible exposure in America. Despite hailing from Seattle, Hendrix (who died in a drug overdose in 1970 at age 27) had already charted in England, but was still largely unknown in the United States. The Monkees would be his last train to hitsville.

When Purple Haze started climbing up the charts, he must have felt enough was enough. He quit the Monkees tour after one last gig at Forest Hills Stadium in New York, where he reportedly flipped the bird at the restless teenyboppers in the stands. Chandler would later write the whole experience off as one big publicity stunt.

This was a drag for Dolenz and the other Monkees, who would arrive early and stand in the wings just to watch their opening act warm up. Noted Nesmith: "I stood in front of the stage and listened to Hendrix at sound check. And I thought, 'Well, this guy's from Mars; he's from some other planet, but whatever it is, thank heaven for this visitation.'"

Still, even they had to admit the odd booking just didn't make sense. As Tork observed, Hendrix was playing "screaming, scaring-the-balls-off-your-daddy music compared with The Monkees." Dolenz sympathized with parents who had to sit through a "god-awful" Monkees concert after seeing "this black guy in a psychedelic Day-Glo blouse, playing music from Hell, holding his guitar like he was fucking it, then lighting it on fire."

In one final twist, Hendrix's abrupt departure from the tour (which also featured The Sundowners and Australian singer Lynn Randell on the bill) was explained in a mock press release that became accepted as fact. Music critic Lillian Roxon concocted the ruse, stating Hendrix was kicked off the tour after the right wing group Daughters of the American Revolution complained his act was "too erotic" for the impressionable young audience. Many press organizations ran with the prank and a genuine Monkee myth was born.

CHAPTER 11

Final Jeopardy: Game Show Myths and Rumors

Okay, couples, here's the 25-point bonus question. If you were an urban legend, and you wanted to spread like wildfire, where is the likeliest place you would start?

Yes, television is correct, but a more specific answer is on a game show. Think about it. Game shows, which have been around as long as network television itself, are the original reality shows, giving ordinary citizens a taste of TV fame as well as a shot at instant fortune and riches. The game show phenomenon really started on radio, where depression-era audiences sat mesmerized at the opportunity to win enough money to buy a house, a car, or even simply pay the rent.

The giddiness of the era is reflected in films like Preston Sturges's *Christmas in July* (1940), when a neighborhood goes nuts after an honest and generous (if cynical) working stiff finally wins a $25,000 jackpot—he thinks. That film (and Sturges's earlier play, which premiered shortly after the 1929 stock market crash) is all based on a hoax. Our hero (played by Dick Powell) wants to believe he has written a winning coffee company slogan ("It's not the coffee keeping you up at night, it's the bunk"). Some wise guys at the office work up a fake telegram declaring him the winner. Before the contest organizers catch up to the lie, the winner goes out and buys presents for all the kids on his street.

Even though the premise seems farfetched and ridiculous, it is nevertheless believable. There was something about radio that fueled imaginations and ignited word of mouth—two elements essential to any urban legend.

Some of these actual game show rumors and legends have their roots in radio. Others sprang from the disillusionment that set in after the game show scandals of the '50s, when the American public's eyes were opened after it was revealed contestants were fed answers in advance on popular shows like *Twenty-One*, *Dotto*, and *The $64,000 Question*. Suddenly, on television, any lie was plausible and any truth was in doubt.

The silliness of such '60s shows as *The Dating Game* or *The Newlywed Game*—two of producer Chuck Barris's wild concoctions—pushed the envelope as to what TV could get away with in terms of content. Voyeurism and exhibitionism were suddenly given a national platform. People weren't just "making whoopee" behind closed doors, they were talking about it in daytime and in prime time. For better or worse, Barris proved there was no shortage of people willing to be exploited or humiliated on television.

The Gong Show was the ultimate wake up call. Dismissed at the time by critics as proof TV really was a wasteland, it was simply, as frequent judge Arte Johnson said, "an amateur hour for people with no talent."

Thirty years later, it still resonates. As game show historian Steve Beverly says, NBC's 2006 summer hit *America's Got Talent* "is nothing more than *The Gong Show* on steroids." What are popular relationship shows like *The Bachelor* and *Blind Date* then but *The Dating Game* on Viagra?

Perhaps more than in any other genre, the line between fantasy and reality is blurred on game shows. Here are a few of the most persistent game show rumors and urban legends. As usual, the truth behind the stories is often more bizarre than the tales themselves.

RUMOR: Newlywed Game *host Bob Eubanks once asked, "Couples, where is the most unusual place you've ever made whoopee?" A woman replied, "That would be in the butt, Bob."*

TRUE: Eubanks once offered a $10,000 reward to anyone who could prove the above exchange actually happened. Late night talk show host Jimmy Kimmel, among others, took him up on it, insisting it not only happened, but was broadcast on TV. Time to get to the, uh, bottom of this.

Created by notorious quiz show producer Chuck Barris (profiled in George Clooney's 2003 movie *Confessions of a Dangerous Mind*), *The Newlywed Game* has logged nearly 20 seasons in various network and syndicated runs. The original daytime version began in 1966 and ran through 1974. A prime time version was spun off from 1967 to 1971. The series surfaced again in the late '70s, '80s, and '90s in syndication.

Eubanks, a former Los Angeles DJ famous for booking The Beatles into the Hollywood Bowl as well as pushing the limits of hair spray to new heights, became a familiar face as the host of the series. Critics assailed *The Newlywed Game* when it premiered in 1966 for dragging standards down to a new low. At the time, *TV Guide* called it, "the worst piece of sleaze on television today."

Naturally, it was extremely popular. The suggestive questions were part of the show's tacky charm. Eubanks admits that he often asked, "Where's the weirdest place you ever got the urge to make whoopee?" on the show and that he got many hilarious replies. "Whoopee" was reportedly the least offensive substitute for sex ABC censors would allow at the time. It became such a *Newlywed Game* catchphrase that Eubanks stuck with it into the later incarnations of the series into the '80s and '90s when he could have come straight out and asked, "Couples, where's the weirdest place you ever did it?"

Viewers came to expect the racy double entendres. Two other examples actually used on the series: "Husbands, how much would you say your wife's chest weighs?" and "What will your husband say is his least favorite condiment on his wiener?"

While there were many silly and sometimes salacious answers, for years Eubanks insisted that no one ever said, "That would be in the butt, Bob." In a 1997 *Entertainment Weekly* interview, he stated, "It never happened. No matter where I go, it's mentioned three or four times a day. Everybody swears they saw it. I'm going to write a book and call it *That Would Be in the Book, Bob.*"

Well, it's in this book, Bob. GSN (formerly The Game Show Network) did unearth a bleeped clip from a 1977 "Maternity Day" episode in which a woman named Olga did give a similar, more vulgar, answer to that very same question. Here is the exchange:

Eubanks: Here's the last of our five-point questions. Girls, tell me where, specifically, is the weeeeeiirdest place that you personally, girls, have ever gotten the urge to make whoopee. The weirdest place. Olga?
Olga: Umm... (audience laughter) [pause]
Eubanks: Yes, Olga?
Olga: Uh...
Henry (her husband): Go ahead.
Eubanks: Yes, Olga.
Olga: I'm trying to think. Umm... [Turns to husband.] Gee Henry, what did you say?

Eubanks: Hey, don't ask him. He can't help you out at all.

Olga: Is it in the ass? [Last three words bleeped]

Eubanks: No no no…no…what I'm talking about is the weirdest location, the weirdest place…

Olga: The weirdest location. I don't know. [Laughs]

Henry: [Laughs uproariously]

That is likely the source of the story, although, despite what Kimmel says, there is no way that the exchange ever actually made it to air back in 1977. No ifs, ands, or butts.

The word "butt" was also not used in this exchange, perhaps letting Eubanks off the hook for that $10 grand payout. Still, the legend is essentially true; a woman gave a similar answer during an actual taping of the show, even if she didn't use the words "butt" or "Bob."

Where and how people first saw it is another matter. Eubanks told *TV Guide* in 1999 that the "weirdest" story he had ever heard was that the clip was part of a training film for the Albuquerque police department.

While that seems unlikely, I can recall renting a "Game Show Bloopers" videotape from a store in the San Fernando Valley in the mid-'80s that had the infamous clip on it. (The same tape also has the clip from *The Price Is Right* where the woman popped out of her halter top as she "came on down" the aisle for Bob Barker.) It also turned up, along with censored gaffes from *Star Trek* and *Happy Days*, in a 1989 video titled *Blushing Bloopers*.

The urban legend–debunking site Snopes.com has been running a clip of the exchange since 2000. NBC aired the same clip in February of 2002 on their special, *The Most Outrageous Game Show Moments*. Eubanks, who reluctantly presented the clip, simply said he'd forgotten the incident when asked about it on that same special. It was also featured in *Confessions of a Dangerous Mind*.

Eubanks finally did write *It's In the Book, Bob!* (with Matthew Scott Hansen), which was published in 2004. That "In the butt, Bob," crack? Just plain forgot about it, repeated Eubanks, who refused to be interviewed for this book.

For the record, hubby Hank guessed Olga would say that the weirdest place they ever made whoopee was in the car on the freeway. Their children must be very proud.

RUMOR: *Game show executive producer Chuck Barris (The Newlywed Game, The Gong Show) was a paid assassin for the CIA.*

RIDICULOUS: *Barris, who, with* The Dating Game *and* The Newlywed Game *proved people would do anything to get on TV, also proved people would believe any-*

thing when he wrote his unauthorized autobiography, Confessions of a Dangerous Mind.

In the 1983 book, Barris said that, during trips overseas when he was chaperoning *Dating Game* contestants, he did double duty as a CIA hitman, notching over 100 kills. The 2002 movie based on the book, which was directed by George Clooney, suggested Barris pulled the trigger on 33 kills.

Either way, the legend sticks because of that age-old urban myth truism: if you're going to lie, make it a truly outrageous whopper. Then it will seem like it could not have been made up.

Barris's associates seem only too happy to keep the myth alive. "Chuck did a lot of traveling, and he had, you know, guns under his bed, so who knows," Barris Enterprises executive Vince Longo said in the 2006 GSN documentary, *The Chuck Barris Story: My Life on the Edge.* Clooney says he approached making the film as if he was a lawyer and he was trying to make a case. "He was a game show host during the day and a CIA agent at night," Clooney said.

On the same GSN special, Barris himself says he simply gets a kick out of the fact that this question even exists. "This book has a premise, you either buy it or you don't buy it, and that's that. I'll never admit to anyone as long as I'm around whether I was or I wasn't," he says, "because I don't think the reader cares other than if you read *Confessions* and you enjoyed it, then that's good."

One guy not buying it is longtime *Newlywed Game* host Bob Eubanks, who was quoted as saying, "If he was a CIA assassin, than I'm Mary Poppins." 'Course, keep in mind that this is the same guy who swore up and down that "in the butt, Bob" never took place.

RUMOR: A woman with 19 children once appeared on the '50s' quiz show You Bet Your Life. *"Why do you have so many children?" host Groucho Marx asked. "It must be a terrible responsibility and a burden." The woman said, "Because I love my husband." To which Groucho replied, "I love my cigar, too, but I take it out of my mouth once in a while!"*

UNSUBSTANTIATED: Groucho Marx said many witty and spontaneous things during his lifetime, including one of my favorites, "Quote me as saying I was mis-quoted." He also said, "Outside of a dog, a book is a man's best friend. Inside of a dog, it's too dark to read."

But did he ever say, "I love my cigar, too, but I take it out of my mouth once in a while?" It sure sounds like something Groucho would say, which is why it is right to be suspicious. Almost every witty quote anyone said in the twentieth century has been at one time or another attributed to the Marx brother with the loping gait and the big black moustache.

The fact is, a lot of Marx's witty rejoinders were penned by great playwrights and screenwriters like George S. Kaufman. "Go, and never darken my towels again," and "I worked my way up from nothing to a state of extreme poverty" came from a movie, not from Marx's fertile imagination.

Although, left to his own devices, he could shoot from the lip with the best of them. Groucho himself tells this story (in *The Marx Brothers Scrapbook*, a rambling and at times obscene record of an elderly Groucho reminiscing) of Kaufman attending a rehearsal for one of their Broadway shows. Suddenly, during the show, Kaufman shushed Alexander Woolcott, the noted theater critic. Sorry, said Kaufman, "I thought I heard one of the original lines."

If only Kaufman had attended the taping of Groucho's radio and TV hit *You Bet Your Life* the day the famous exchange about the lady with too many children and the cigar supposedly took place. The show had the simplest premise imaginable: Groucho sat on a stool and chatted with a variety of guests pulled out of the studio audience. He basically asked questions until somebody said the secret word, then a duck with a Groucho moustache came down with a check for a hundred dollars or some such smallish amount. NBC promoted the series in the mid-60s with the line, "One man on a chair has drawn more viewers over the last six years than any other attraction on television." That the series lasted 14 seasons (11 on television) is all due to Groucho. Viewers tuned in each week to see what outrageous thing he'd say next.

A bit of a controversy erupted during the run of the show when it was revealed that there were two writers on staff and that Marx could refer to a crude kind of TelePrompTer. Still, Groucho never met the guests before the show and most of the rejoinders were true ad libs spun off of what a contestant happened to be saying.

It's doubtful a writer could have fed Groucho this exchange:

Groucho: Where are you from?
Young woman: I'm from Ralph's grocery store.
Groucho: You were born in a supermarket, eh? I thought supermarkets
                didn't make deliveries anymore. Oh, you're the cashier? Now
                it's beginning to register.

So it is entirely plausible that this great comedian could have come up with the cigar line at the drop of an ash. But did he? In his book, *Raised Eyebrows: My Years inside Groucho's House*, author Steve Stoliar suggests that it happened but never aired. Stoliar, a college student who met Marx and, in the comedian's final few years, became his secretary and archivist, checked into the story with various surviving *You Bet Your Life* producers.

One of them, head writer Bernie Smith, kept track of each and every contestant who had ever appeared on both the radio and TV versions of the show. "There was, it seems, a sign painter named Mr. Story from Bakersfield, California," wrote Stoliar. The man and his wife had what was reputedly at the time to be the largest family in America, with 22 children, although three had died. Mrs. Story was picked to appear on the radio show. Her conversation with Groucho supposedly went like this:

Groucho:	How many children do you have?
Mrs. Story:	Nineteen, Groucho.
Groucho:	Nineteen?! Why do you have so many children? It must be a terrible responsibility and a burden.
Mrs. Story:	Well, because I love children—and I think that's our purpose here on earth—and I love my husband.
Groucho:	I love my cigar, too, but I take it out of my mouth once in a while.

Stoliar recounts that the studio audience roared with laughter, but director Bob Dwan ordered the exchange cut before the program went to air. This was easy enough to do; Dwan, who directed and later edited all the shows, told Stoliar that they always shot about an hour of material before editing each episode into a crisp half hour.

Unfortunately, no recording of the exchange, even as an outtake, exists. It never went over the radio, so only studio audience and crew members, besides Groucho and the woman, would have heard the line. It certainly never aired on TV, so anyone who claims they saw it is mistaken.

Marx himself, who died at the age of 86 in 1977, both confirmed and denied that the exchange ever took place. In 1972, in an *Esquire* article, he told film critic Roger Ebert that "I got $25 from *Reader's Digest* last week for something I never said. I get credit all the time for things I never said. You know that line in *You Bet Your Life*? The guy says he has seventeen kids and I say, 'I smoke a cigar but I take it out of my mouth occasionally?' I never said that." Then, just four years later, in his book, *The Secret Word Is Groucho*, he claims he did say it. "The story," he wrote, "is not apocryphal. It did happen." Marx claimed the studio audience roared, but director Dwan, who Marx refers to as "the house censor," clipped it out of the broadcast.

While that could be exactly what happened, Groucho's keen mind was starting to wander in the last year of his life (when *The Secret Word Is*

Groucho was published). This whole anecdote could have been ghostwritten or just prompted by Stoliar's digging.

In his 2000 memoir, *As Long As They're Laughing*, Dwan said he didn't personally remember the cigar crack, but later became convinced it happened after consulting with Smith, who shared the same information he told Stoliar: it took place during a radio taping, was never broadcast, and that "it was never heard outside the confines of NBC Studio C in Hollywood."

This still sounds fishy to the folks at Snopes.com, who note that Dwan found no hard evidence of the exchange in the "collection of acetate recordings of the unedited performances and tapes of the edited broadcasts" or even on the four reels of 16mm film containing "the funniest and most audacious of the sequences which we were required to delete from the broadcasts as being unsuitable for viewing in the 1950s."

It is certainly unlikely the line would have slipped past the censors. Even a more harmless response, like this from a contestant, was edited for air. Here, Groucho asks a man to recount his most embarrassing moment. "I was rooming with a 300-pound fellow," the man said. "And the bedroom caught fire. In my panic, I put on the big fellow's trousers and shoes. I was coming down the ladder when a shoe came loose. I tried to retrieve it, and I dropped the trousers. There was a crowd of 500 people below, and they could see my predicament."

That exchange was preserved on tape by NBC editors, but primarily because they wanted to save the huge laugh that came afterwards. It was used for years to "sweeten" the audience response to other jokes on the show.

There is recorded proof that exchanges like the cigar line took place on *You Bet Your Life*. In 1955, Groucho was interviewing a mother and daughter. There were 17 children in the family. When the daughter explained that her daddy loves children, Groucho replied, "I love pancakes, too, but I haven't got closets full of them."

Groucho also once asked a father of triplets what he did for a living. The man answered that he worked for the California Power Company. "My boy, you don't work for the California Power Company," Groucho cracked, "you *are* the California Power Company!"

RUMOR: Days after Hurricane Katrina leveled New Orleans, the game show The Price Is Right *offered an all-expenses trip to the city.*

TRUE: Some game show legends are just actual occurrences that sound like stuff somebody made up. An overly excited woman once really did pop right out of her halter top after being told to "Come on down!" on The Price Is Right. *"That actually happened," says Bob Barker, who finally stepped down as host of* The Price Is Right *in 2007 after 35 years on the CBS daytime classic. "I was behind the door, I hadn't been introduced yet," Barker told me in January of 2007. The network actually ran with the boob boo-boo (this was two decades before Janet Jackson's Super Bowl boob flash), with a banner superimposed across the woman's breasts. (You can look it up on YouTube.)*

Barker took the stage but had no idea what had just happened. He recalls then-announcer Johnny Olsen bellowing, "Bob, she has given her all for you!"

The Price Is Right also got tripped up in the wake of Hurricane Katrina. On September 8, 2005, 10 days after Katrina struck with catastrophic results and with evacuations still underway, a repeat episode of the daytime game show offered contestants "a round-trip coach from Los Angeles to New Orleans for a six-night stay at the Renaissance Pere Marquette Hotel, within walking distance of the French Quarter."

The episode dated back to December, 2004. CBS officials pulled it before it ran in the Pacific time zone, but it already aired in the Eastern, Central, and Mountain zones. The network issued an apology and vowed to screen the content of all future programming to avoid further embarrassment. "Our thoughts and prayers are with the brave citizens of the Gulf Coast," said CBS spokeswoman Beth Haiken in a statement.

Never a rumor, just bad luck and coincidence.

RUMOR: A contestant on the game show Press Your Luck *won over $110,000 in prize money by memorizing the patterns of the prize board's sequence of lights.*

TRUE: On May 19, 1984, Michael Paul Larson, an unemployed ice cream truck driver from Ohio, rang up the largest win in the history of the game show Press Your Luck: *$110,237. This stood for years as the biggest TV game show win in one sitting. Keep in mind, this was 15 years before* Who Wants to Be a Millionaire *and* Greed *ramped game show winnings into million-dollar heights.*

Press Your Luck pitted three contestants against a giant electronic board. After answering questions correctly in an early round, the players earned chances to take "spins" on the big board. It consisted of 18 squares containing either cool prizes, cash, or the game-ending "whammy," an animated gremlin which took away all of a player's accumulated winnings, reducing their total to zero.

As documented in the 2003 GSN special, *Big Bucks: The* Press Your Luck *Scandal,* Larson arrived at the taping with a carefully calculated plan. For eight months, he studied the show at home and hooked up a VCR to record episodes. In this way, he was able to break down the board action frame by frame, dissecting the patterns. After weeks and weeks of study, he deduced that there were just six predictable patterns to the electronic game board. He memorized the sequences until he knew he could stop the board on prize winning squares, completely avoiding the dreaded whammy.

Larson borrowed money for airfare to Los Angeles and tried out for the game show. His audition went well but contestant coordinator Bob Edwards had doubts. "There's something about this guy that worries me," he told executive producer Bill Carruthers, who repeated the story in a 1994 TV Guide article. "I overruled him," said Carruthers. "I should have listened to Bob."

Wearing a 50-cent shirt he had just purchased at a thrift store, Larson was booked on the show where he faced off against a returning champ (who had won $11,000 up to that point) and a dental assistant. He hit a whammy on his first spin, flunked out by buzzing too early on an easy money question ("Franklin D. Roosevelt's likeness is on the head side of what American coin?"), and generally did not distinguish himself on the first round. By the second round, however, where the board came into play, Larson put all his weeks of rehearsal and observation into practice. Instead of hitting a whammy once every six spins (as most contestants would do if playing randomly), Larson sailed through 40 consecutive winning spins. He kept landing in the "Big Bucks" square, racking up between $3,000 and $5,000 at a time.

Host Peter Tomarken started freaking out when Larson went beyond the $25,000 total and did not pass. Everyone figured the dude's luck would soon run out and he would get whammy'd down to zero.

While the other two players watched and the studio audience cheered, Larson spun on to $40,000, $50,000, and $60,000 in winnings. By the $70,000 mark, he seemed to tire of the constant winning and nearly blew it all, missing the stops he had in mind by buzzing in a split second late—but still lucking out by landing on trips and other lesser prizes instead of the whammy.

When he cracked the $100,000 mark, Larson finally passed on to the other players. The studio audience gave him a standing ovation. The other two players took a few turns and the pass came back to Larson. He hit for cash twice more, then nearly blew it all by stopping one frame early, narrowly missing a whammy and netting a trip to the Bahamas instead. Larson passed, the dental assistant struggled, and Larson ended the hour the new champion with $104,950 in cash, a sailboat, and trips to Kauai and the Bahamas. "How does it feel to be part owner of CBS?" quipped Tomarken.

It was a staggering amount at the time. By contrast, Charles Van Doren, the quiz show cheater who electrified and then shocked America on *Twenty-One* in the '50s, took 15 weeks to win $129,000.

Scared that they had another quiz show scandal on their hands, the producers huddled with CBS and their lawyers immediately after the taping. Bottom line, Larson had done nothing illegal. There was no rule against paying attention. Larson was allowed to take home his full share of the prize money. He was, however, banned from returning to the series.

After Larson's record run, the producers scrambled to prevent someone else from taking them to the cleaners. They rewired the electronic game board, adding about 20 more random patterns. A cap of $75,000 in winnings was imposed. Nobody else was able to pull a Larson for the remaining two years the show was on the air.

Unfortunately, Larson's luck really did run out after his game show triumph. About $35,000 of his winnings went to pay taxes. A chunk was invested in a real estate deal that quickly went bust. He then withdrew his remaining winnings, between $40,000 and $50,000, from his bank in a doomed effort to win a further $30,000 in a radio contest (the idea was to match a dollar bill's serial number with one read out randomly at the station). According to his wife at the time, who appeared on the GSN special, Larson became obsessed with the radio contest, repeatedly withdrawing and depositing his winnings in an effort to get different serial numbers. The move backfired as the money was stolen from his house. Shortly after, his common-law wife left him.

Just two years after his big win, Larson was wiped out. He begged to go back on the show. It was too late anyway—*Press Your Luck* was canceled in 1986.

Larson didn't even get to relive his moment of glory on television. CBS and the producers were so embarrassed by the way they were played they withheld the two episodes featuring Larson for 19 years. GSN finally got permission to show them in March of 2003, when their *Big Bucks* documentary aired. Larson told his rags to riches to rags story to *TV Guide* and *Good Morning America* in 1994 when Robert Redford's somewhat related *Quiz Show* movie revived interest in his exploits. Five years later, in 1999, he was dead, a victim of throat cancer. At the time, he was on the run from the U.S. Securities and Exchange Commission.

Whammy.

CHAPTER 12

Too Much Drama: Urban Legends about Drama Series

The final scene in *The Sopranos* probably ranks as TV's greatest head scratcher. What happened? Who turned out the lights? Did Tony and his family get whacked right there and then in that restaurant or did they all live happily ever after?

Immediately after the finale aired on June 10, 2007—or at least once the shock wore off—people began speculating about what happened next. If series creator David Chase had wanted to launch a thousand TV rumors and myths, he couldn't have written a better ending.

Chase clearly knows that great TV drama is as much in the mind as it is on the page. Respectful of his audience, he allows viewers to fill in the blanks. Many went so far as to post their version of what happened next on the Internet.

Not all the drama in this chapter aims as high as *The Sopranos*. For example, what do Ed Asner, Pamela Anderson, and David Hasselhoff all have in common? Anderson and Hasselhoff, that's easy, both were on *Baywatch*. Asner? Definitely never played a lifeguard.

Still, all three have starred in more than one TV series over the years and most of those were dramas. Asner, in fact, may hold the record for most series roles, with the short-lived 2006 to 2007 drama *Studio 60 on the Sunset Strip* being at least his 12th series credit. Along the way, from *The Mary Tyler Moore Show* to *Roots*, he's won seven Emmys, more than any other male performer.

Hasselhoff? Not so many Emmys. Same with Anderson. But, really, would a book about TV's greatest urban legends make any sense without Pamela Anderson or David Hasselhoff? Would any book about anything?

RUMOR: *Ed Asner was so convincing as gruff news editor Lou Grant, a real newspaper offered him a job editing their paper.*

TRUE: *But only for a day.*

Asner played gruff-but-loveable Lou Grant for 14 seasons on two series, *The Mary Tyler Moore Show* and *Lou Grant.* He is the only actor to have won Emmys for Best Comedy and Best Drama acting honors for playing the same character.

I spoke with Asner in 2004 when he was promoting his 11th TV series, the short-lived CBS comedy *Center of the Universe.* "Toronto Sun?" said Asner, noticing my name tag at the CBS press tour event. "I used to run your newspaper. Is Peter Worthington still in charge of the place?"

A relatively recent *Sun* hire at the time, I was unaware that Asner had once barked orders at *Sun* staffers. A check back at the office, where Worthington, the paper's founding editor, was still pounding out commentary as a columnist, confirmed that Asner had been editor for a day 25 years earlier, in 1979.

Like most newspaper people, Worthington and *Sun* publisher Doug Creighton had been big fans of Asner's realistic newsroom drama *Lou Grant.* They decided to try and lure him across the border to run the paper for a day, mainly as a publicity stunt. Worthington flew to Los Angeles to make the pitch.

Asner, as it turned out, was scheduled to be in town anyway to shoot a movie (Toronto gained a reputation as "Hollywood North" in the late '70s/early '80s thanks to tax incentives and a cheaper Canadian dollar). So not only did he agree to Worthington's offer, it didn't cost the *Sun* a cent to fly Asner north.

Well known as a Hollywood liberal, Asner was certainly at odds with the *Sun*'s right wing newsroom at the time. Still, he was the *Sun*'s guest of honor at the Canadian National Newspaper Awards after his first day on the job.

Just the same, the *Sun* fired him the next day. The crime, according to Worthington: "Being a TV character."

What were the actor's memories of the experience? "It was pretty larky," said Asner—proof enough for me that he really did work at the *Sun.*

RUMOR: *Former* Baywatch *babe Pamela Anderson was originally supposed to play the Teri Hatcher role on* Desperate Housewives.

FALSE: Talk about desperate. This rumor was started by Anderson herself. In a 2004 interview with the New York Post, *the balloon-breasted actress claimed she turned down the chance to play suburban housewife Susan Mayer—the part that eventually went to Teri Hatcher—on the ABC series. "Now I could kick myself as the show is simply great," she told the* Post.

Why did she turn it down? According to Anderson, it was because the producers wanted her to have brown hair. "Blonde is my trademark so I said no," she said. "I am hoping to persuade them to give me a guest star role."

When asked about Anderson's statement, however, *Desperate Housewives* creator and executive producer Marc Cherry was unequivocal. "No offer was tendered," he told TV critics gathered at a 2005 press tour session in Los Angeles.

That certainly doesn't mean Anderson wasn't considered for the role. As Bill Carter chronicles in his 2006 book, *Desperate Networks*, "actresses all over Hollywood were practically crawling into Touchstone on their bleeding knees to audition for these meaty, mature women's roles." Cherry himself confirmed that Heather Locklear was considered for one of the four main women, but, while Cherry and his partners dithered, she signed on as one of the leads of NBC's short-lived drama *LAX*. Oops.

Another actress who claimed she could have been a desperate housewife was Sela Ward. "I was sent the script," said Ward. "It was the Teri Hatcher role." While Ward was careful to explain that no firm offer was on the table, she insisted she was a contender. Fresh off her own series, *Once and Again*, and also dealing with the recent passing of her mother, Ward was less than anxious to commit to another hour-long drama. While she admitted that she regretted "not being on a show that successful," she did later land a recurring role on another hit, the medical drama *House*.

According to Carter's book, there was enough resistance to Hatcher from the network and the studio to leave the door open to several other actresses. Hatcher's star had faded since her breakout days playing Lois Lane on *Lois and Clark: The New Adventures of Superman*. As she approached 40, she couldn't even keep her gig playing opposite football commentator Howie Long in a series of Radio Shack commercials.

It was an all too familiar scenario in Hollywood, wrote Carter: "Sexy young thing of limited range ages past her sell-by date and can't get arrested." There were also doubts Hatcher could pull off the physical comedy as well as the full dramatic range that went with her klutzy, vulnerable character. Hatcher, however, aced her network audition and resurrected her career.

Carter names dozens of other actresses who tried out for *Desperate Housewives*. Mary Louise Parker and Calista Flockhart, wrote Carter, were also both considered for Hatcher's Susan role. Dana Delany, Roma Downey, Jeri Ryan and Sharon Lawrence were all in the running to play Bree, the part won by Marcia Cross. Even Nicollette Sheridan tried out for Bree, but, at the suggestion of director Charles McDougall, wound up with the role of Edie, or, as Sheridan referred to the character, "the slut."

While she turned down the part of Bree, Delany eventually did land on Wisteria Lane, joining the cast in the fourth season in September, 2007 as the wife of the town gynecologist (played by Nathan Fillion). "You only get second chances two times in life," Delany told me at the July, 2007 press tour.

Cherry was convinced that the easiest role to cast would be that of the youngest housewife, Gabrielle. The part called for a Hispanic and a model, which would narrow the search down, he reasoned. "There aren't that many people writing leads for Latina females."

That's when his casting director said, "You want her to be gorgeous and to be able to act and do comedy. You're going to get three people audition-ing." Cherry says he lucked out because one of them was Eva Longoria, although, again, according to Carter, Rosalyn Sanchez was in the running.

Carter also names Jeanne Tripplehorn and Alex Kingston as desperate to be *Housewives*. He further claims Julia Louis-Dreyfus pursued the Susan role, but Louis-Dreyfus herself shot that down at a press tour session for the launch of her CBS comedy, *The New Adventures of Old Christine*.

While there were many actresses who were either turned down or passed over for *Desperate Housewives*, the biggest pass had nothing to do with cast-ing. NBC Universal chair Robert Wright admitted his network turned down the entire series. ABC got it and briefly bounced to the top of the pack, while NBC tumbled down to fourth place among the networks.

RUMOR: David Hasselhoff is a huge recording star in Germany.

TRUE: Okay, maybe not Elvis huge, but he was very big in Germany in the '90s.

Certainly his music is far more popular in Europe than it is in North America. The former *Knight Rider* lead, who is mainly of German ancestry, was already a popular recording star in Austria and Switzerland when, in 1989, he decided to cover a German hit from the '70s titled "Auf der Strasse nach Süden."

Retitled "Looking For Freedom," the catchy pop anthem coincided with the political changes sweeping through Eastern Europe at the time. A month after the Berlin Wall was smashed down in November of 1989, Hasselhoff was invited to headline a New Year's Eve concert at the historic site. He stood atop a partially demolished section of the wall and belted out the lyrics: "I've been looking for freedom/I've been looking so long/I've been looking for freedom/still the search goes on."

The ballad struck a chord with Germans frustrated with years of division. Hasselhoff recalled that "close to a million East and West German fans stood together in the freezing cold at midnight watching me perform. I was overcome with emotion."

At this point, Hasselhoff was making a huge TV comeback as "the hunk in the trunks," lifeguard Mitch Buchannon, on the worldwide hit *Baywatch*. That action hour, about a group of amazingly hot lifeguards (featuring spectacular *Playboy* pinup Pamela Anderson), was reportedly seen in over 140 counties. At the height of *Baywatch*'s global popularity, *The Guinness Book of World Records* declared Hasselhoff "the most watched TV star in the world," pegging *Baywatch*'s weekly worldwide audience at over 1.1 billion viewers.

Evidently some of those viewers bought CDs. Many lived in Germany. The *Looking for Freedom* album topped the German charts for three months and the single stayed number one for eight straight weeks.

Hasselhoff scooped up several German music awards for *Looking for Freedom* and went on to become one of the top recording stars in Germany during the '90s, reportedly outselling artists such as Madonna. It all led to this actual headline appearing in a German newspaper—"Hasselhoff: Not Since The Beatles."

Still, this all seemed like a joke to many in North America, where Hasselhoff was never much of a recording star. An attempt to launch his music career there through a live, 1993 pay-per-view special was derailed when O.J. Simpson's infamous white Bronco chase broke the same day. Even *Baywatch* was lightly regarded in North America as a breezy "jiggle" show where Hasselhoff was overshadowed by Pamela Anderson's breasts.

Norm MacDonald, who anchored *Saturday Night Live*'s satirical "Weekend Update" segment during much of the '90s, would often end a report on *Baywatch* with the phrase, "Which once again proves my old theory, Germans love David Hasselhoff."

Hasselhoff was frequently the butt of jokes on late night talk shows. Conan O'Brien once cracked, following an impaired driving charge leveled against the former *Knight Rider* star, that the police could tell something was up because his talking car was slurring its words.

Instead of being insulted by the jokes, the six foot four actor rolled with the ribbing. "I'm a big punching bag," Hasselhoff told TV critics at a 2006 press tour session for *America's Got Talent*, a reality show featuring the entertainer as one of three judges. "I just kind of go with the flow." A turning point, he said, is when he winked at his reputation in the 2004 comedy *Dodgeball*, playing the uptight coach of a German team. That cameo led to an appearance (in swim trunks, no less) in *The SpongeBob SquarePants Movie* (2004).

Embracing his campiness has paid off handsomely for "The Hoff" and probably furthered his recording career. A "Get Hasselhoff to number one" Web site helped propel his 2006 single "Jump in My Car" to No. 3 on the UK charts by that October.

Bottom line, we're not sure about some of Hasselhoff's other claims, such as being the most Googled star on the planet (typing in his name in a 2006 Google search did fetch an impressive seven million plus hits) or about single-handedly ending the Cold War. (Hasselhoff griped to *Spielfilm* magazine in 2003 that his Berlin Wall stunt was a turning point. "I find it a bit sad," he said at the time, "that there is no photo of me hanging on the walls in the Berlin Museum at Checkpoint Charlie."

What we can say for sure is what Norm MacDonald always insisted: "Germans love David Hasselhoff."

RUMOR: On just about every episode of Dragnet, *Sgt. Joe Friday (Jack Webb) uttered the famous line, "Just the facts, ma'am."*

FALSE: Just as Humphrey Bogart never said, "Play it again, Sam," in Casablanca *and Cary Grant never said, "Judy, Judy, Judy" in any movie, Webb never uttered the line that is so associated with his popular police drama.*

Dragnet, which was created by Webb, began its long run on radio in 1949 before moving to television in 1952. It stayed on NBC until 1959 and was later revived as a color series from 1967 to 1970, with Webb back as no-nonsense police detective Joe Friday.

Friday was steadfastly polite. The Los Angeles police detective was always saying, "Yes, ma'am," or, "No, ma'am." Parents would hold him up as an example to their kids.

Dragnet was an instant smash, with its distinct, "Dum-dee-dum-dum" opening theme repeated everywhere. The realistic drama was the number two series during the 1953 to 1954 season, behind only *I Love Lucy*.

It was so successful that it inspired a parody comedy record by humorist Stan Freberg that itself became a million seller and number one hit. Goofing on *Dragnet*'s dryly intoned opening narration, the parody, "St. George and the Dragon," started with, "The legend you are about to hear is true. Only the needle must be changed to protect the record." The recording got even more exposure when Freberg was invited to perform his parodies on Ed Sullivan's popular Sunday night variety show, *Toast of the Town*.

The routine on the flip side of the record was titled "Little Blue Riding Hood" and it was here that the phrase Friday was supposed to have always said was born. After Little Blue Riding Hood says, "Why Grandma, what big ears you've got!" Freberg's Sgt. Wednesday says, "All the better to get the facts, ma'am. I just want to get the facts, ma'am."

That somehow got shorted in people's minds to, "Just the facts, ma'am." What Webb would sometimes say on the series was more along the lines of, "All we want (or all we know) are the facts, ma'am."

Yet it was Freberg's phrase that stuck, just as "Judy, Judy, Judy" caught on after Cary Grant impersonators started using the line. With myth and legend, it seems, imitation is indeed the sincerest form of television.

RUMOR: Robert Young, who played Marcus Welby, MD, for seven seasons in the '70s, went blind after the series went off the air.

FALSE: Already a TV legend for his six seasons on Father Knows Best *(1954–60), Young came out of retirement at age 62 to play kindly doctor Marcus Welby. He was paired opposite James Brolin, who played hip, chopper-riding Dr. Steven Kiley.*

The hour-long series was an old-fashioned hospital drama that clicked with viewers, ranking as the most-watched show in all of television for the 1970–71 season.

Young, who appeared in 100 movies throughout the '30s and '40s, became so identified with his later TV role that some people actually believed he was a doctor. This impression was further cemented after Young appeared in a long-running series of aspirin ads wearing a white lab coat. As the old ad saying went, he wasn't a real doctor, but he played one on TV. That was enough for most consumers, who trusted that Robert Young would never steer them wrong.

The characters Young played, especially on television, always seemed smart and affable, real down-to-earth, guy-next-door types. The truth was that Young suffered for years from depression and drank to excess to cover a painfully shy and insecure personality. "All those years at MGM," he once said, "I hid a black terror behind a cheerful face."

Between his two hit series, he appeared in a short-lived flop, *Window on Main Street*. Afterwards, he had a nervous breakdown. It took him years to recover enough to try acting again. *Marcus Welby, M.D.*, marked a triumphant return.

Still, dark clouds followed Young even into later life. In 1991, as he grew older and struggled with the onset of Alzheimer's disease and heart problems, he even tried to commit suicide.

Given this dichotomy between Young's TV persona and his personal life, it is perhaps not so surprising that wild rumors began to crop up about the actor. Young was quite candid about his depression in his later years, hoping his story would encourage other people to seek help. The Robert Young Center for Community Mental Health, based in Rock Island, Illinois, salutes the fact that Young helped raise funds as well as awareness for the cause.

With awareness, however, sometimes comes confusion. Lurid tabloid headlines alluding to Young's mental health problems helped create the notion that the actor had a secret. For some reason, a rumor began to circulate in the early '80s that he had gone blind.

At the time, Young, who would continue to work well into his eighties (he died in 1998 at 91), was appearing in a series of commercials for Sanka brand decaffeinated coffee ("97% caffeine free"). The tip-off that he was blind, according to the persistent rumor, was that he always had his hand on someone in those commercials.

As Hal Morgan and Kerry Tucker wrote in their 1984 book *Rumor!*, "this one rates several stars for sheer silliness." Sure, Young was blurring the line between fantasy and reality. He was using his image as a trusted authority figure to sell aspirin and decaffeinated coffee. Father knows best, especially when he is a doctor.

But blind? Because he sometimes rested his hand on somebody's shoulder? Maybe it was just karma getting back at Young. The lesson: never try to cash in on your TV fame. Blind faith is not something to be trifled with.

RUMOR: Tony gets whacked at the very end of the series finale of The Sopranos. *You can tell because of who was in the diner at the time, and because of a conversation Tony had earlier in the season with his brother-in-law, Bobby.*

FAGETABOUTIT: The heart pounding, mystifying Sopranos *finale already has become one of the most talked about moments in the history of television. New Jersey mob boss Tony Soprano (James Gandolfini) is sitting with his wife Carmela (Edie Falco) and son "A. J." (Robert Iler) at a local diner. Their daughter Meadow (Jamie-Lynn Sigler) is outside struggling to parallel park her car. Various shady characters enter the diner. In a scene right out of* The Godfather, *one suspicious gent heads to the washroom. As Tony's jukebox selection, Journey's "Don't Stop Believin'" blares, the scenes cut back and forth from the street to the diner to Tony's eyes. Just as he looks up to see who has entered the diner, the screen goes black. The end.*

What the...? HBO's Web site got so many hits that night from angry, confused viewers that it crashed. Fans got no answers from David Chase, the creator and executive producer who wrote and directed the episode. He was in France, far from the furor. The only thing he did say, to columnist Alan Sepinwall of the *Newark Star-Ledger* (the hometown paper often found at the end of Tony's driveway), was "Anybody who wants to watch it, it's all there."

That's when the rumors really started to fly. A viral e-mail message was circulating the day after the finale ended stating it had proof that Tony was dead. All you had to look at was who was in the diner at the end, the author of the e-mail argued. The menacing guy at the counter was Phil's nephew, out for revenge. (Wrong—the person who played this part, Paolo Colandrea, is listed in the credits as "Man in Members Only Jacket;" this was his first acting job ever). Two men who tried to kill Tony in season one are seen entering the restaurant. (Impossible—Tony killed at least one of those guys in that early episode.)

Other theories, including one from a widely read Web posting, centered on a conversation Tony had earlier in the season with his brother-in-law, Bobby (Steve Schirripa). "You probably don't even hear it when it happens, right?" was Bobby's view of death. There was no sound of a gunshot at the end of *The Sopranos*, therefore Tony is dead, went the theory.

And on and on it went. The finale was dissected for religious imagery (one shot of Tony in the diner supposedly was framed to look like the Last Supper), references to *The Godfather* and other possible clues. It was pointed out that Tony was shot in an earlier *Sopranos* episode titled "Members Only"—proof that the guy in the Members Only jacket pulled the trigger.

Among the most ridiculous rumors swirling after the finale was that the guy in the Members Only jacket was played by Journey frontman Steve Perry. Another was that, in fading to black for ten long seconds, Chase had killed the entire audience!

There is no denying that this was the most anticipated series finale since *M*A*S*H* went off the air in 1983. Chase had at least a year to figure out how he was going to end his masterpiece. All those choices in the diner had to have been deliberate. If those suspicious-looking guys were not thugs from earlier episodes out for revenge, why tease viewers into thinking they were? Why all the red herrings and build-up? Was it strictly to create tension?

Perhaps. Chase insisted in a statement that he was not "trying to be audacious, honest to God. We did what we thought we had to do. No one was trying to blow people's minds, or thinking, 'Wow, that'll (tick) them off.'" He was not trying to mess with viewers, he was simply trying to entertain them.

About a month after the episode aired, after most of the furor had died down, Chase flew in to Los Angeles from France to accept two honors at the annual Television Critics Association awards. Critics hoping he might finally spill the beans about the ending were quickly brought back to reality. "Here's another clue for you all," said Chase in accepting the first award. "The Walrus was Pauly."

If you are a Beatles fan, you probably recognize the reference to a lyric in "Glass Onion" that supposedly commented on those long ago "Paul McCartney is dead" rumors. The fact was Paul wasn't dead and Beatles fans had simply let their collective imagination run wild. Chase seemed to be saying that *Sopranos* fans were doing the same thing by overly deconstructing the ending.

In accepting his second award of the night, Chase concluded with a anecdote about seeing the original "Planet of the Apes" movie back in 1968 when he was a graduate student at Stanford University. "Wow, so they had a State of Liberty, too," was Chase's complete misread of that ending.

"That's what you are up against," Chase told critics. Everyone is going to have their own read on what happened and some of us are going to be completely wrong.

Whatever. Maybe *The Sopranos* simply ended on a family moment, going out, as *Toronto Star* critic Rob Salem wrote, "not with a bang, but with a dinner." Let it go, and pass the cannoli.

CHAPTER 13

Reality: What a Concept: Reality Show Rumors

Reality TV may have diluted TV's ability to convey truth to the point where we just don't believe anything anymore. After several years of *Joe Millionaire*, game playing on *Survivor*, and phony romances on *The Bachelor*, what are a few more rumors or urban legends but just more blended reality?

Would Arnold Schwarzenegger get elected Governor of California without three seasons of *Survivor*? After all, what is *Survivor* or *American Idol* but an election, held every seven days, with somebody being tossed away like a week-old sandwich? Who wouldn't want to do the same to dull and ineffective politicians? Sooner or later, the idea had to spread to what was once known as the real world (before the MTV reality show *The Real World* blurred that, too). Like the California recall vote, *Survivor* is a popularity contest. People win by staying under the radar, by not taking a stand, by being as charismatic and inoffensive as possible—in short, by being Schwarzenegger.

With reality shows like *The Apprentice*, *American Idol*, and *Fear Factor* becoming the new entertainment, there's more fantasy to be found in reality. Schwarzenegger launched his campaign from Jay Leno's couch on *The Tonight Show*. (A trick he learned from Bill Clinton, who got a leg up on the Oval Office from *Arsenio Hall*). Immediately after the election, it was Leno who introduced the Governor at his victory party. Former *West Wing* insider Rob Lowe stood on the stage, not as an actor in a political drama, but as a Schwarzenegger adviser. Blurry enough for you?

Just remember that circus slicker P. T. Barnum, the guy who said, "There's a sucker born every minute," was a Republican member of the Connecticut state House of Representatives.

I'm just glad *Smothers Brothers'* clown Pat Paulsen ("If nominated I will not run; if elected, I will not serve") isn't around for any of this. The poor sap might have gotten elected.

At least Paulsen, who died in 1997, didn't have to witness the dark side of the reality circus, when humiliation and embarrassment disguised as entertainment directly or indirectly led to heartbreak, jail time, and even death. They don't call it *Survivor* for nothing.

RUMOR: Original Joe Millionaire *Evan Marriott was not an unemployed contractor, as the network claimed, but actually the heir to the Marriott hotel chain fortune.*

FALSE: The FOX network described lanky impostor Marriott to viewers as a 28-year-old construction worker making $19,000 a year. On the hugely popular 2003 reality series, he posed as a wealthy playboy who had inherited $50 million and longed to share it with a fabulous babe. Twenty single women traveled to France to compete for his phony fortune. The press had a field day, dubbing Joe Millionaire *"the ditch digger meets the gold diggers." More than 40 million viewers tuned in to the finale, ranking it at the time as the highest-rated FOX TV show ever.*

The rumor that Marriott might actually be rich began while the show was still on the air. FOX teased viewers that one more big twist was coming in the finale of the show. Many thought that it would be revealed that he really was wealthy. No such luck, Marriott told TV critics. "All those people who (speculate about his wealth), where were they when I was eating beanie wienies morning, noon, and night?" he said at the time.

Besides a little underwear modeling (thesmokinggun.com revealed that, two years before *Joe Millionaire*, needy Marriott had posed in swimwear and thongs for a California company), the Virginia Beach native claimed he made $30 an hour digging pools and at other odd jobs. He didn't have a lower-class background, however. Marriott's father was an investment banker and his mother worked in high-end retailing. "I grew up with nice things," he said in a 2003 interview, "and although, like everyone else, I like money, I don't see the point of too much of it."

Paul Hogan, the dapper Australian who played Marriott's butler on the series (and who was a butler in real life as well as a former attaché to the Australian embassy in Canada) said, rich or poor, Marriott was a stand-up guy. "I've met many Evan Marriotts in my life," said Hogan. "He's a construction worker, he's good-hearted, he's warm, he's generous, he's got a good sense of humor, enjoys a beer, likes fast food. He's a good bloke." He was also very easy to work for, says Hogan. "He wasn't demanding in any way. In fact, he was prepared to carry my suitcase!"

Marriott did wind up wealthier once the show ended. He split one million bucks with his chosen woman, Zora Andrich—who took her share of the money and ran. Which makes sense considering the reality behind the outcome of this so-called reality show—Marriott didn't really choose his chosen, she was chosen for him. "She was chosen because she was the right one for the show rather than for me personally," he explained later. "She really didn't care about the money and that was what they wanted."

"They" are the producers and the network with whom, Marriott says, he clashed frequently. They kept trying to sex up the series, editing in scenes and sound effects to suggest Marriott had a tryst in the woods with runner-up Sarah. That's the girl he would have chosen, by the way. "We got along just great and had great conversations," he said.

After his 15 minutes of *Joe Millionaire* fame were up, Marriott briefly hosted the reality dating show *Fake-a-Date*, did a cameo in a cable TV movie, and shot a few ads for KFC and Ragu. At last report, he was back in the construction business, running his own contracting company in California.

RUMOR: Rudy Boesch, the gruff but loveable ex-Navy SEAL from the first edition of Survivor, *only made the final four after interference from executive producer Mark Burnett.*

FALSE: Whether or not there was any attempt to keep him in the game, there's no denying that Boesch was one of the most popular players in Survivor *history. The grizzled combat veteran stood out not just in age (at 71, he was the oldest* Survivor *player), but also in attitude. "If they listened to me, they'd all have haircuts," he snorted during the very first episode of the series.*

Boesch, however, did not wind up as *Survivor*'s first winner. That distinction went to Richard Hatch, the openly gay corporate trainer who eventually went to prison after failing to pay taxes on his million-dollar winnings.

The rumor that the original *Survivor* was somehow "fixed" to keep Boesch in the game began to spread shortly after the series ended, when a lawsuit was filed by another contestant. Stacey Stillman, a San Francisco–based lawyer who was ousted early in the contest, charged that executive producer Mark Burnett had a hand in her exit from the island.

As part of her deposition, Stillman filed testimony from another player, Dirk Been, who said that around the ninth day of the competition, Burnett suggested a "keep Boesch, ditch Stillman" strategy. At the next tribal council, Stillman was eliminated in a five to two vote, with Been among those voting against her.

Burnett denied the accusation, testifying that "at no point during the production of *Survivor* did I . . . ever direct any of the participants to vote for or against a particular participant, or attempt to manipulate, coerce, induce, intimidate, or influence the participants' voting."

Burnett had previously volunteered that he had staged scenes on *Survivor* with stand-ins for better camera shots. A river swimming race during the second installment, for example, was later reenacted with stand-ins so a helicopter crew could get better shots. CBS just saw it as better story telling, saying viewers knew the challenges and emotions were all real. Nothing Burnett did affected any outcomes, they felt, including Boesch's advance to the finals.

Stillman's allegations were repeated in author Peter Lance's book, *The Stingray: Lethal Tactics of the Sole Survivor*. In an interview with the *Toronto Sun* in 2003, Lance called *Survivor* "the *Twenty-One* scandal of the decade," a reference to the quiz show scandals of the '50s. The judge hearing the Stillman case didn't agree, throwing out the complaint. In the court of public opinion, moreover, Stillman came off as a sore loser.

Boesch, on the other hand, won far more than the $85,000 he pocketed as *Survivor*'s first third-place finalist. The retired Navy SEAL made dozens of personal appearances, was introduced as a war hero in the Virginia House of Delegates, was honored with a "Rudy Boesch Day" at a military base, and even worked as a consultant for Burnett on other reality projects.

Still, a whiff of scandal occasionally still lingers over *Survivor*. More hearsay emerged during the tax fraud case of Hatch, where his lawyer, Michael Minns, alleged that Hatch caught his fellow reality show contestants cheating. (Specifically, that "friends" were somehow sneaking other players food onto the remote Borneo island where *Survivor* was shot.)

According to Hatch, he took this information to the producers and struck a deal; they would pay the taxes if Hatch won the million-dollar first prize. Burnett testified at the trial, but, curiously, was not asked about any tax deal with Hatch. The judge sided with Burnett, convicted Hatch of tax evasion, and sentenced the original *Survivor* winner to more than four years in prison for, among other things, lying "repeatedly."

CBS has always stood by their executive producer. "I can tell you there was no producer manipulation in *Survivor*," said Chris Ender, senior vice president of communications. "There are so many crazy things written about *Survivor* that we think our viewers will recognize that they shouldn't believe everything that they read."

As host Jeff Probst would say, "The tribe has spoken."

RUMOR: An unsuccessful contestant on The Contender *committed suicide after being bumped from the show.*

TRUE: This was never really a rumor, just a sad fact. Najai Turpin, a 23-year-old from Philadelphia who was one of 16 fighters vying for a million-dollar purse on NBC's boxing reality series, shot himself in the head just weeks before it premiered.

While Turpin didn't win, his brother told *Access Hollywood* that the suicide was unrelated to the outcome of the reality series, which was another Mark Burnett production. "The show was never the problem, boxing and all of that was never the problem. It was a personal problem," said Diediera Turpin.

Turpin's body was found in a parked car in front of a local gym. Nearby was the home of his girlfriend and their two-year-old daughter.

"All of us at *The Contender* mourn the loss of a great fighter with tremendous heart and courage," said Burnett in a release. Coexecutive producer Sylvester Stallone said, "Najai embodied the *Rocky* spirit as a Philly fighter from humble beginnings." Footage featuring Turpin remained in *The Contender* and a trust fund was later set up for his family.

RUMOR: A contender on the original Swedish version of Survivor *who was despondent at being the first person voted off committed suicide.*

TRUE: The original version of Survivor, *called* Expedition Robinson, *was made for Swedish television. It was a hit in that country in 1997. It was, however, also marred by an early tragedy—the suicide death of Sinisa Savija, the first contestant to be voted off the island by his peers.*

On July 11, 1997, just before the series premiered, Savija threw himself in front of a train. *Survivor* producer Mark Burnett did not produce this series, but did address the tragedy, saying that Savija, a Bosnian refuge, had a history of psychological problems.

Survivor has always had strict rules about eligibility, including one question on the contestant form which asks, "Have you ever been treated for any serious physical or mental illness(es) within the last three years?"

Savija's widow contended that her husband had become despondent over his abrupt departure from the show and was worried about others seeing his failure on the air. She quoted her husband to the Associated Press, saying, "They are going to cut away the good things I did and make me look like a fool, only to show I was the worst and that I was the one who had to go."

Savija's death isn't the only suicide connected to participation in a reality show. Besides boxer Najai Turpin's suicide prior to the premiere of *The Contender*, there was Melanie Bell, a TV producer who jumped to her death from the top of a Las Vegas hotel after taking part in a reality show called *Vegas Elvis*. In England, a 17-year-old was found hanging from a tree after returning from four months in Australia where she was taking part in a reality show called *The Colony*. (The British History Channel series had various family members assuming pioneering roles as Australian colonists.) The British teenager was reportedly despondent after "coming out" as a lesbian on the series.

In 2005, a woman who was the sister of a participant on ABC's *Extreme Makeover* took her own life. Kellie McGee—who was struggling with bipolar disease—was one of several family members who were asked to point out the physical flaws of her sister, Deleese Williams, on camera. Their comments would later be edited in as Williams underwent various forms of plastic surgeries designed to correct her crooked teeth, deformed jaw, and small breasts.

Except the producers decided to dump Williams on the eve of her life-changing surgeries. She was told to go back home to Texas. Guilt-ridden over her comments, McGee moved out of the home she shared with her sister and brother-in-law, and four months later, died from an overdose of pills, alcohol, and cocaine.

TV isn't always pretty.

RUMOR: *The Bachelor, Aaron Buerge, got three contestants from the show pregnant.*

FALSE: *This one circulated on the Internet in the form of an e-mail immediately after Buerge's* Bachelor *finale aired in 2002. The rumor was sent out in the guise of an AP wire report, making it sound official:*

New York (AP)—What was expected to be a storybook ending for ABC's popular *The Bachelor* series tonight erupted into a full-fledged scandal when network executives and the show's producer confirmed following this evening's season finale that three women had allegedly become impregnated while on the show by Aaron Buerge, 28, the show's featured bachelor.

The hoax e-mail went on to quote Michael Eisner—then CEO of ABC's parent company, Disney—demanding Buerge take a paternity test and ensuring viewers he'd "get to the bottom of this."

While the e-mail was riddled with spelling mistakes (including Buerge's name), not to mention the world's longest and clumsiest lead, the salacious nature of *The Bachelor* made it sound at least halfway believable. For eight weeks on TV, Buerge, a 28-year-old Missouri native who was the second "Bachelor," basically smooched his way across America with two dozen humiliated hotties before narrowing his choice down to either Helen Eksterowicz or Brooke Smith. In the ponderous two-hour finale, he slipped a ring on Eksterowicz's finger.

Like almost all these romantic reality shows, the instant pairing never took. Five weeks after the finale aired, Eksterowicz told the real Associated Press that she was dumped at a Starbucks near her New Jersey apartment. "It felt like a bomb dropped," the 28-year-old elementary school psychologist told *People* magazine. She felt "deceived" and told Buerge, "You've told me every single day that you love me, and now this is it?" One silver (or gold) lining: Eksterowicz kept her two-carat diamond engagement ring.

The "reality-show-stud-gets-reality-babe-pregnant" theme is a steady product of the TV rumor mill. Everybody but that old coot Rudy has been accused of getting busy on *Survivor*. And don't even get me started on *Temptation Island*.

Another *Bachelor* rumor had it that the original dude, 31-year-old management consultant Alex Michel, was pressured into picking the underdog in the finale of the series by ABC. As reported by the *New York Post*, this rumor started as a hoax. Seems Michel initiated an e-mail chain encouraging some old Harvard pals to watch the show, in which he picked younger Amanda Marsh over former Miami Heat cheerleader Trista Rehn (who would go on to become ABC's first *Bachelorette*). A friend of a friend of Michel's then circulated a fake e-mail supposedly from the unsuspecting bachelor suggesting he picked the "fatter" of the two finalists and that the producers made him pick the underdog. "Don't worry," Michel then supposedly wrote, "I bagged Trista."

The real author of the e-mail, Jon Locker, came clean to the *Post*, admitting "it was a complete hoax and I feel really bad about it." Ironically, there were reports later that Michel really did have second thoughts about picking Marsh and that he continued to contact Rehn even before he split with his chosen one. Ah, romance.

RUMOR: *American Idol loser William Hung died from a heroin overdose.*

FALSE: *Talk about wish fulfillment. Hung, a 21-year old University of California, Berkeley, student, shattered nerves and eardrums all over North America after botching Ricky Martin's "She Bangs" at a 2004 Idol audition.*

News of Hung's "death" started out as a prank on the Internet satire site Broken Newz. "The announcement of his death sent shockwaves to the tens of people who still found him funny," went the posting. Hung's spastic rendition of Ricky Martin's "She Bangs" so horrified *Idol* scrooge Simon Cowell he begged the kid to stop.

Hung's plea that he had never had a lesson was such a howler that he at least stood out from the parade of other desperate pop wannabes. Overnight, he was the Hong Kong Ricky Martin, as proclaimed on his Web site (williamhung.net). He went on to release a best-selling CD (hilariously titled *Inspiration*), destroying such pop standards as "Hotel California," "Can You Feel The Love Tonight," Rocket Man," "Circle of Life," "YMCA," and "Shake Your Bon-Bon."

By becoming more popular than any of the *Idol* finalists, Hung has erased any doubt that the show is anything but a karaoke contest. When I interviewed him in 2004, he was busy shooting his first video (for "She Bangs") and only had about four minutes to talk. "What can I do? Everyone wants a piece of me," he said. "That's cool, that means I'm popular, you know?"

RUMOR: CBS cheated Amazing Race *contestants Rob Mariano and Amber Brkich out of a sure win by having a flight delayed in the last leg of the race, allowing good guys Uchenna and Joyce Agu to get on the same plane and beat the former* Survivor *lovebirds to the finish line.*

UNSUBSTANTIATED: "I saw what all of America saw," was Mariano's answer in early 2007, when asked about this persistent Amazing Race *rumor.*

After racing across five continents and more than 40,000 miles, the seventh edition of *The Amazing Race*, which aired in the spring of 2005, came down to front-runners Rob and Amber with what seemed like an insurmountable lead with the last leg of the race to go.

A million dollars was at stake. "Amber and I were on that plane spending the money," says Mariano. "In all the years of my life I've never seen a plane come back."

What really happened with that American Airlines flight from San Juan, Puerto Rico, to Miami? Here are the facts: the plane was already running late when Rob and Amber scrambled aboard. Uchenna and Joyce were at first told they had missed the scheduled 10 A.M. departure and booked themselves on the 11:15 flight. When they noticed that the 10 A.M. flight still hadn't left the ground, they lobbied the gate attendants to call the pilot to grant permission for them to sneak onto the earlier flight.

It happens. Uchenna and Joyce had no bags to check. They bought a pricey, last minute ticket. Pilots do have the discretion to open the plane for one or two more passengers. What is more unusual is the fact that the door had been sealed shut and the commercial jet had actually started to pull away. Uchenna and Joyce must have been pretty persuasive—or somebody at American Airlines saw an incredible marketing opportunity. (Mariano later pointed out that American Airlines was an *Amazing Race* sponsor.)

CBS said it had nothing to do with Uchenna and Joyce's good fortune (and CBS's good fortune—having the two top couples on the same plane led to a down-to-the-wire finish). "Only an understanding gate agent and the goodwill of the pilot returned the Jetway back to the plane," said a CBS spokesman. "Uchenna and Joyce treated everyone with kindness and respect throughout (the) race, and that karma was returned at a crucial moment."

The other key fact is that the race was still up for grabs when the plane the two teams were on touched down in Miami. A wrong turn in a cab ride is what eventually cost Rob and Amber the race.

For Marino, nicknamed "Boston Rob" and "The Rob Father" after practically narrating *Survivor: Marquesas*, this was the second time he had placed second in a televised race to a million. At least the last time he got to share the wealth, proposing to Brkich just as she was declared the winner of *Survivor: All-Stars*. Brkich had previously competed in *Survivor: The Australian Outback*.

Throughout their *Amazing Race* run, the couple constantly traded on their reality show fame, grabbing preferential treatment from cabbies and pedestrians along the route. It did seem as if their good fortune simply ran out at the very end of the race. Perhaps karma had caught up to them, too. Rob's aggressive game playing and cockiness rubbed some viewers the wrong way, especially when he and Amber sped past fellow racers Brian and Greg, who had been in a car accident. All the other teams checked in on the unlucky brothers.

"America can judge," Mariano was content to say when he and Amber guested on *Live with Regis and Kelly* shortly after their *Amazing* adventure ended.

He also admits that "CBS has been good to us." Right after *The Amazing Race* ended, the network aired a two-hour *Rob and Amber Get Married* wedding special. Shortly after I spoke with them in January of 2007, the couple competed again in a brand new all-star edition of *The Amazing Race*. And while they were eliminated early, they got a few more exotic trips to far-flung places out of the bargain.

One way or another, it looks as if Rob and Amber are going to make up for that lost million.

RUMOR: American Idol *judge Paula Abdul slept with one of the contestants on the series.*

UNSUBSTANTIATED: *This wasn't just a rumor, this was a full-blown scandal. It was tabloid fodder for months and even inspired a competing network's prime time news special.*

The *Idol* rumor began after 2003 contestant Corey Clark alleged that he had a sexual relationship with Abdul during his aborted run on the series. (Clark, who made it through to the final 12 singers, was kicked off the show for not coming clean about earlier charges he once assaulted his younger sister.) He also alleged that Abdul helped him prepare for his performances, picked out his clothes, and essentially coached him through the series.

Abdul, through a spokesman, quickly countered that Clark was "an admitted liar and opportunist" who was "communicating lies about Paula Abdul in order to generate interest in a book deal."

Clark sang to ABC News, which blew the story wide open when it aired *Primetime Live: Fallen Idol*, billed as "a startling look behind the scenes" of the hit reality series. The special aired in May of 2005, just prior to that season's *Idol* finale. (Fierce competition between the networks had led to a "gloves off" policy, especially after FOX tried to blunt ABC's *Wife Swap* and *Supernanny* earlier that same season with blatant copycat shows *Trading Spouses* and *Nanny 911*. In TV, revenge is a dish best served during sweeps.)

After first trying to joke away the controversy, the FOX network protected its biggest hit by conducting their own internal investigation into the alleged affair. An independent counsel was hired to look into Clark's damaging claims. FOX entertainment president Peter Liguori told reporters that both Abdul and Clark were interviewed along with "corroborating witnesses." The counsel's not-so-surprising conclusion—there was no proof that Abdul had an affair with Clark. As *New York Times* columnist Bill Carter noted in his book, *Desperate Networks*, the internal investigation "helpfully absolved Abdul by saying the kid's claim could not be proved."

The network did, however, impose an "enhanced non-fraternization policy" in order, they said, to prevent future incidents that could call the relationships between judges and contestants into question. "I'm grateful this ordeal is over, and I'm so looking forward to getting back to the job I love," Abdul said in a statement issued after the FOX announcement.

She made few other statements, ducking out of a January 2006 TV critic's press tour session, leaving her *Idol* colleagues to clean up her mess. Asked about the fallout from the internal FOX investigation, judge Randy Jackson joked that he "can't touch Simon anymore." As in Simon Cowell, *American Idol* and FOX's highest-paid star, who put the whole sleazy matter in perspective: "I love controversy," he told critics. "I hope there is more."

RUMOR: *A Dutch reality show offered participants a chance to win kidneys and other human organs.*

FALSE: *The story made headlines around the world in May of 2007.* The Big Donor Show, *a reality series which aired on the Dutch network BNN, was going to pit three contestants against one another for the express purpose of winning much-needed human organs from a real live donor.*

The news shocked even the prime minister of Denmark, Jan Peter Balkenende, who condemned the producers. So did the Royal Netherlands Medical Association, which questioned the ethics and even the viability of such an outrageous enterprise (donors and patients have to be carefully matched and screened) and urged its members not to participate in the series.

What they were reacting to was an actual TV show. A Dutch woman, identified only as Lisa, was said to have inoperable brain cancer and was willing to donate her organs through a TV contest. Contestants vied for the chance to impress her and win one of her kidneys.

On the final episode of the series, it was revealed that it was all a hoax. "Lisa" was an actress and no human organs were really being awarded. The three contestants on the show were all in on the gag, which was odd, considering all three really desperately needed organ donations.

The host of the show, Patrick Lodiers, later said in a statement that the whole idea was to raise awareness about the very real need of organ donations and, specifically, about the plight of these three people. The show aired on the fifth anniversary of the death of the founder of the TV network, Bart de Graaff, who lost his life after waiting seven years for an organ donation.

The series hailed from Endemol, the Dutch production house behind such internationally successful reality shows as *Big Brother* and *Deal or No Deal*. Officials there insisted the intention all along was simply to draw attention to a very real need, which, it could be argued, they succeeded in doing.

CHAPTER 14

So Not Dead: TV Stars Who Supposedly Died but Didn't

Mark Twain said it best: "Rumors of my death have been greatly exaggerated."

Actually, he never said that, but it sounds better than, "The report of my death was an exaggeration."

In any event, the saying could apply to Paul McCartney, Abe Vigoda, Richard Dawson, or any of a dozen other famous people who had supposedly died in a tragic bathtub accident or were found dead from a heroin overdose.

Often rumors of the death of a TV star crop up after they haven't been seen for a few years. Once-hot stars like *Saturday Night Live*'s Joe Piscopo, *Max Headroom*'s Matt Frewer, and *Blossom*'s Mayim Bialik have all been subjected to premature obits. Former *Boy Meets World* star Ben Savage supposedly died in a drunk driving car accident in September of 2006, a baseless rumor that apparently started out as a hoax on Myspace.

The fascination with death and celebrity has even led to "Dead Pools," sites where you can log on and confirm or deny the latest on who is or isn't "late."

One of the biggest names in the history of show business was once erroneously reported dead. Bob Hope was still celebrating his 95th birthday when an obituary for the famous comedian somehow popped up on the Associated Press site. Arizona Republican congressman Bob Stump got up in the House of Representatives in Washington and said, "It is with great sadness I announce that Bob Hope has died."

And that's how rumors start, folks. Somebody gets the wrong information and blabs all about it at the wrong place at the wrong time. The news quickly spread to C-SPAN and other news outlets before Hope's daughter Linda contacted various agencies to say her dad was happily having his breakfast at his home in Toluca Lake, California.

Hope lived to be 100, passing away in 2003. Shortly before he died, his wife asked him where he wanted to be buried. Said Hope, "Surprise me."

The following rumors sure surprised the friends, families, and fans of these individuals—not to mention the individuals themselves.

RUMOR: Bob Denver, from Gilligan's Island, was electrocuted when a radio slipped into his bathtub.

FALSE: This rumor took off even before Denver won the starring role as the bumbling first mate on Gilligan's Island (1965–67). In the late '50s, the New York native became a familiar face as work averse Beatnik Maynard G. Krebbs in The Many Lives of Dobie Gillis (1959–63). It was on this show that Denver's slightly spaced out persona first took root.

For some reason, in and around the time Dobie Gillis went off the air, a rumor spread that Denver had been shocked to death in his bathtub. "The closest we got to tracing it is that some kid in the Midwest had run into a classroom and shouted it," Denver told TV Guide in 1998. After that, he said, the wire services picked up the rumor and it spread all over the country.

Denver said he ran into people for years afterward who couldn't believe he was still alive. "I remember one flight attendant who screamed when she saw me."

That would make more sense now—Denver died on September 2, 2005. There was no radio or bathtub to blame, however, when having just survived quadruple bypass surgery, Denver died from complications related to throat cancer treatment. The Skipper's "Little Buddy" was 70.

RUMOR: Barney Miller curmudgeon Abe Vigoda died in 1982.

FALSE: Vigoda has become the poster boy for "Dead or Alive?" celebrities. This stoop-shouldered New York City native always had such a dour expression that there were people who thought he was dead way back when he played Detective Sergeant Fish on the squad sitcom Barney Miller (1975–82). The character *was always wheezing or complaining. When Fish "retired" from* Barney Miller's *Greenwich Village precinct house in 1977, Vigoda was awarded his own spin-off series,* Fish *(1977–78). It lasted only a season. After that, Vigoda, a busy and popular actor throughout the '70s (he was featured in everything from the ABC soap* Dark Shadows *to* The Godfather*) seemed to disappear suddenly from the small screen, even though he never stopped working. Some people thought he had passed away.*

That included at least one staffer at *People* magazine, where it was erroneously reported in 1982 that Fish was now sleeping with the fishes.

Vigoda, who was born in February of 1921, has always been a good sport about not being dead. He even posed for a *People* magazine retraction photo, which showed him sitting up in a coffin, reading the erroneous magazine report. "I'm flattered that people remember me and think of me," he said in a 2000 interview.

This didn't stop other media outlets from reporting that Vigoda was dead. In 1987, a reporter at a Secaucus, New Jersey, station referred to him as "the late Abe Vigoda." She corrected her mistake on the next day's broadcast.

In 1999, Vigoda had a real life brush with death aboard an American Airlines flight between San Diego and New York. A compressed air line burst at 31,000 feet, causing cabin pressure to drop and oxygen masks to be deployed. The plane was forced to make an emergency landing in Palm Springs, but not before a few of the passengers were slightly injured, including Vigoda.

His "death" turns up as an annual joke on *Late Night with Conan O'Brien*, where he has made dozens of appearances, sometimes tricked up with lights like a Christmas tree. In November of 2006, for example, he turned up in a sketch where someone from the studio audience starts summoning the dead (Vigoda, of course).

The persistent rumor of his death even made it as an entry on *Who Wants to Be a Millionaire*. A contestant was asked, "Of these five celebrities, which one is not dead?" The contestant correctly picked Vigoda, suggesting that the word is finally getting out that this guy is still alive.

The Beastie Boys and others have referred to him in song. In 2002, a Gothic rock group, Galcik, recorded a song called "Abe Vigoda's Dead" (it was a parody of an earlier tune, "Bela Lugosi's Dead"). There's a Web site that has one purpose: to report the current status of the actor—dead or alive. For a while, there was even an "Abe Vigoda status extension browser" set up so that Firefox Internet search users could be constantly reminded of Vigoda's current state of existence.

Vigoda, of course, outlived this little gag, just as he has so many others in the past.

RUMOR: Never mind what the survey says—Richard Dawson is dead.

FALSE: Again, this seems to be a case of a TV star being everywhere for 10 or 15 years and then suddenly slipping under the radar. Out of sight, out of mind, and maybe out of time—everybody thinks you're dead.

Richard Dawson was certainly ubiquitous, enjoying a 20-year run on television, sometimes appearing on two shows at once. The British-born actor first gained fame in America as resourceful Corporal Peter Newkirk for six seasons on the World War II prisoner of war comedy *Hogan's Heroes* (1965–71). At the end of the '60s, he was also cast as a panelist on the daytime game show *Match Game* (1969–81). The show went on to become the number one show on daytime television. A prime time version was spun off, with Dawson emerging on both shows as the star most players singled out for the "super match" segment at the end of each round.

While Dawson was popular with viewers, he wasn't with everybody on the show. Some were jealous of his breakout success, if fellow panelist Brett Somers's comments are any indication. "I remember he left the show and everybody was thrilled," Somers remarked on the 2006 GSN documentary, *The Real Match Game Story: Behind the Blank*. Occasional panelist Betty White was a little more diplomatic. "His mind worked like a steel trap," she said, "but he wasn't the happiest man in the world."

There are suggestions that Dawson felt above the show when it started to take off in the mid-70s. He lobbied producer Mark Goodson for his own series and got it—*Family Feud* (1977–85), which was essentially spun off from *Match Game*'s "super match" clue board. For a season or so, the former *Hogan's Heroes* actor was starring twice a day on two different game shows.

By 1977, it was clear even to viewers that Dawson didn't want to be on the *Match Game* panel any more. The producers came up with a spinning wheel to try and give the other celebs a shot at some face time during the big money guesses, something Dawson took as a personal affront. In protest, he began wearing tinted glasses and whispering his answers. The producers gave him his release. "I moved on to greener pastures," he said on the GSN special.

It was true at first. *Family Feud* quickly took over the number one daytime ranking. Dawson's "Survey says!" became an instant catch phrase. His habit of kissing every single female player on the show was also part of *Feud*'s corny charm. By the mid-80s, however, hour-long soaps had squeezed many of the game shows off the network schedules. *Feud* ended its run in 1985.

When it returned in a new syndicated version in 1989, Dawson was replaced with a new host, Ray Combs. A standup comedy booking on *The Tonight Show Starring Johnny Carson* launched Combs's TV career. He did so well his first time out the studio audience gave him a standing ovation. Impressed, Carson helped Combs land other jobs.

Landing the revived *Family Feud* gig was the high and low point of his career. While he was able to follow in Dawson's large footsteps, ratings eventually went down and, in a last ditch attempt to save the series, the producers bounced Combs in 1993, bringing back Dawson as host. (The attempt fizzled; the show only lasted another year.)

Combs had other troubles. An Ohio comedy club he invested in went bankrupt. A car accident in 1994 nearly left him paralyzed. He had recently separated from his wife Debbie—the couple had six children—when, on September 2, 1996, while being treated at a California psychiatric wing, he used bedsheets to hang himself in a closet. It was his wife's 40th birthday.

Combs died penniless; Carson reportedly donated the money to pay for his funeral.

Combs's tragic death may have triggered confusion with as well as rumors of Dawson's demise. There was another lurid angle to the Dawson rumor—that he died after catching a fatal disease from kissing all those strangers on his game show. (No joke: Dawson's death rumor began to emerge shortly after Rock Hudson's death from AIDS-related illnesses in 1986—the year after Dawson disappeared from the screen.)

In any event, Dawson, semiretired and well into his 70s, insists he is alive and well and definitely not dead.

RUMOR: *Former* Happy Days *and* Joanie Loves Chachi *star Scott Baio died in a 1997 car crash.*

FALSE: *Again, this one began as a phony e-mail posting, which suggested Baio died in a car crash on December 18, 1997. (Creepy coincidence: that happens to be the same day comedian Chris Farley died.)*

According to an article in the *New York Times*, the rumor really upset his family. "My parents called me, crying," he said. "They heard it from my brother who heard it on the radio. And they're crying and I'm thinking, 'Somebody in my family died!' Little did I know it was me."

While he jokes about it now, having his parents think he was dead for 30 minutes was no laughing matter at the time. How did the rumor get started?

Baio told *TV Guide* in 1999 that the story he heard was that a body was brought into a morgue "and somebody said, 'Hey, it looks like Scott Baio.'"

Again, out of sight in Hollywood equals must be dead. Like Dawson, Baio seemed to disappear after many years on one of TV's hottest shows, *Happy Days* (1974–84). He followed that with his own spin-off, *Joanie Loves Chachi* (itself the basis for one of TV's funniest rumors—see the "Naked Truth" howler in chapter six).

Over the next decade or so, Baio worked on the forgettable sitcom *Charles in Charge* plus several failed pilots. A few seasons as a doctor on the older-skewing drama *Diagnosis Murder* (1993–95) didn't really raise his profile among his original fans. As far as they were concerned, if he wasn't dead, his career was.

Baio was a good sport about it, leaving a message that he wasn't dead on his answering machine. He bounced back with a role on the final season of *Arrested Development*, playing a lawyer representing the wacky Bluth family by the name of Bob Loblaw (it sounded like "Bla-bla-bla"—get it?).

Baio's casting was all part of the joke. His character took over from the Bluth's previous lawyer, played by his old *Happy Days* mentor, Henry Winkler. (*Arrested Development* was produced—and narrated—by another *Happy Days* grad, Ron Howard.)

Asked for this book if the Fonz was ever dogged by rumors or urban legends, Winkler replied, "Yeah—people believed I was taller."

The Baio rumor may finally be put to rest with the success of VH1's *Scott Baio is 45…and Single*, a surprise cable hit in the summer of 2007. The reality series took its cue from Baio's real life prowess as a ladies' man (Pamela Anderson, Nicolette Sheridan, Brooke Shields, Denise Richards, and Heather Locklear have all been linked to the former *Happy Days* star). The original idea for this series, however, would have reignited the "Scott Baio is dead" rumor. VH1's initial plan was to shoot a mocumentary, starring Baio, based on the real life magazine hoax centered around another former TV teen, Adam Rich from *Eight Is Enough* (see the child stars chapter). VH1's original title for the series? *Let's Kill Scott Baio*. Good thing his mom never saw that in a TV guide listing.

RUMOR: *Steve Burns, the original host of the children's show* Blue's Clues, *died of a drug overdose.*

FALSE: *This is another one of those "innocent-kiddie-show-has-disturbing-secret" rumors that has dogged everything and everyone from Captain Kangaroo to Mr. Rogers. As we grow older, and perhaps more jaded and cynical, some of us seem only too ready to believe the worst about our beloved childhood idols.*

Born in 1973, actor/singer/guitarist Burns began hosting the puzzle-solving Nickelodeon series *Blue's Clues* in 1996. Preschoolers took to the play-along series, with live-action host Burns interacting with a bright blue animated puppy named Blue.

So how and why did the Internet rumor start that he had a heroin addiction? It might have had something to do with an appearance Burns made on the long-running crime drama *Law and Order*. On an episode that first aired on April 19, 1995, he played an autistic teen who seemed strung out on drugs. With *Law and Order* rerunning endlessly, it is possible that kids and parents were alarmed to see their pal from *Blue's Clues* in such a sinister light. The fact that the character died on the show—in the eye-catching sequence before the opening credits—didn't help.

Nickelodeon looked into the story and discovered a Web page that sourced it to a New York radio station. Burns might have simply been burned by some bored and mischievous shock jockers.

In any event, the rumor spread so fast in 1998 that Burns's own mother called to see if he was still alive. Faced with freaking out a generation of toddlers, the producers and the network frantically tried to get the word out to kids and parents that Burns was not some cashed out crackhead. In November of 1998, he was booked on *The Rosie O'Donnell Show* to confirm he was alive and well. An appearance on *The Today Show* followed (where parents were coached on how to explain it all to their kids). Burns made countless newspaper and TV pleas to convince his impressionable young fans he was safe.

The rumor took off again in 2002 when, after six years of dressing up in a green striped shirt and talking to an imaginary salt shaker, Burns quit *Blue's Clues* to concentrate on his music career. At that time, the character Joe (played by Donovan Patton) took over as live action host. Why? Because Burns was dead, or so went the rumor. (Other rumors surfaced that Burns was bounced from the show after a heroin bust or that he had become a porn star. That would be *Blue Movie Clues*.)

The bald truth, as spilled on the Nickelodeon documentary *The 10 Years of Blue*, was that Burns left because he was losing his hair. Teen hosts should be hairier, he figured, handing off to the younger-looking (and not dead) Patton.

Still, the rumor persists. Go to Burns's Web site now (steveswebpage. com), and the first line reads, "not dead, merely decaying..." You can also get caught up there on his current career as an indie rocker. Burns teamed with some members of The Flaming Lips, including drummer Steven Drozd, recorded an album called *Songs for Dustmites*, and is working on future musical goodies.

CHAPTER 15

Didn't You Used to Be What's His Name? A Few Cases of Mistaken Identity

Who wouldn't want to believe that Mr. Green Jeans was the father of Frank Zappa? Or Ted Nugent? Or Alice Cooper? Or any of the other rock 'n' roll riffraff the gentle kiddie show sidekick has been rumored to have sired over the years?

Hugh Brannum, who played Mr. Green Jeans on *Captain Kangaroo* for 30 years, would have to have had some pretty active genes to have lived up to the many urban legends he seems to have spawned.

People seem fascinated by parentage and proximity and opposites attracting and, again, there are enough real life examples to keep even the craziest rumor plausible. After all, Jon Voight did contribute to the conception of Angelina Jolie.

You couldn't get more "out there" than edgy rocker Zappa, a fierce and outspoken nonconformist and proponent of free speech. This is the guy who named his kids Moon Unit and Dweezil. Yet who was his real-life next-door neighbor in the Hollywood hills? Bobby Burgess, the former *Mickey Mouse Club* Mouseketeer and Lawrence Welk dancer.

Mr. Square meets Mr. Dare. You couldn't find two more unlikely neighbors in all of America, yet there they were, side by side, living opposite ends of the American Dream. The idea of Burgess dancing over to borrow a cup of sugar or Zappa walking home with a few Welk albums, well, it sounds like a FOX sitcom. Don't give them any ideas.

Reality show viewers were fascinated to learn that goth rockers The Osbournes lived within ear-splitting distance from classical guitarist Liona Boyd. Hollywood makes for strange bedfellows.

There's also a fascination with stars' past lives—who they were before they made it big. A few years before *The Dick Van Dyke Show* made her a star, a very young Mary Tyler Moore hopped through an appliance ad as Happy Hotpoint. Before he became beloved children's entertainer Captain Kangaroo, Bob Keeshan suited up as the original Clarabell the Clown on *Howdy Doody*. Johnny Carson's sidekick Ed McMahon also started out in TV in clown makeup, slipping on the slap shoes in 1950 for something called *The Big Top*.

That element of surprise and discovery, of finding out who was behind that greasepaint and baggy pants, helps make these other outlandish rumors all the more tantalizing—even if they are completely made up.

RUMOR: *Captain Kangaroo sidekick Mr. Green Jeans is the father of Frank Zappa.*

FALSE: *Prolific musician Frank Zappa inadvertently started this rumor himself by recording two songs linking himself to Captain Kangaroo's laid-back farm pal: "Mr. Green Genes" on the 1968 album,* Uncle Meat, *and "Son of Mr. Green Genes," on his 1969 album,* Hot Rats.

The man was clearly a *Kangaroo* fan. Zappa, who died from prostate cancer at 52 in 1993, addressed the rumor himself, stating, "Because I recorded a song called 'Son of Green Genes'...people have believed for years that the character with that name on the *Captain Kangaroo* TV show (played by Lumpy Brannum) was my 'real' dad. No, he was not."

Hugh "Lumpy" Brannum, who died in 1987, played the role of Mr. Green Jeans on the long-running morning kiddie show from 1955 to 1984. Bob Keeshan—himself the subject of a wild rumor about being a World War II war hero alongside Lee Marvin—played the good Captain.

Brannum, an Illinois native, did have a musical background, playing bass in the '40s and '50s for Fred Waring and his Pennsylvanians. He also did have a son, but it sure wasn't Frank Zappa.

One variation of this rumor suggested that Ted "Motor City Madman" Nugent was Green Jeans, Jr. Hell no. Nugent's father, Warren, was a World War II veteran and later worked for the phone company. He died in 1993. Hard to imagine how growing up with such a kiddie icon for a father would cause you to rebel in such an extreme, opposite direction. Guess it would be a chip off the old rock.

RUMOR: *Josh Saviano, the geeky best friend from* The Wonder Years, *is Marilyn Manson.*

FALSE: And that would make cute little Winnie who then, SATAN? Keep in mind that the late '80s sitcom, The Wonder Years, did begin each week with that blistering rock anthem from Joe Cocker, singing The Beatles' "A Little Help from My Friends." Maybe fans thought that rock 'n' roll spirit rubbed off on a few of the cast members.

Or maybe they just fell for that old irresistible "innocence turns evil" idea. For six seasons, Josh Saviano played Paul Pfiffer, the nerdy pal of the show's grade school protagonist, Kevin Arnold (Fred Savage). Despite all that heavy makeup and that one creepy contact lens, Manson's face actually bears a striking resemblance to Saviano. There are even Web sites where their two faces morph into one.

Manson seemed to welcome the rumor when it surfaced when his career was heating up in the mid '90s. Several other weird rumors followed the singer, including that he had breast implants, a rib removed, and that he replaced an eye with a testicle. So being a nerd on TV? Whatever. "It's kind of irrelevant sometimes whether they're true or not," he once said.

Born January 5, 1969, Manson, whose real name is Brian Warner, is actually seven years older than Saviano (March 31, 1976). An extension of the rumor suggested that Saviano wasn't Manson but the drummer in his band; this is also completely false.

The two did have a close encounter, as Saviano told *TV Guide* in 1999. He and some pals were going to see the rocker when Manson played near Yale's campus in Connecticut. "My friends and I were going to go, because we thought it would be funny with the whole rumor thing," he said, "but it never panned out."

In either event, Saviano is cool with the comparisons. "What would you rather have," he said to *Star* magazine, "people thinking you're a dorky kid from *The Wonder Years* or a satanic rock star? It's way cooler."

Saviano actually wound up going to Yale where he majored in political science. He went on to work as a paralegal in New York before entering law school. He now works as a lawyer in New York.

RUMOR: Alice Cooper played Eddie Haskell on Leave It to Beaver.

FALSE: You can almost hear Mrs. Cleaver now—"Ward, I'm worried about the Beaver's pal Eddie. He just bit the head off a chicken."

Another one you wish was true just because it is so deliciously wrong. The rumor apparently began after Cooper told *Rolling Stone* magazine that he was Eddie Haskell as a child. What he meant was that he was a child of the '50s and that he ran around sucking up to adults, not that he actually was the actor who played Wally's pal Eddie on *Leave It to Beaver*.

Cooper (born Vincent Damon Furnier), of course, always knew the value of rumors. There were several rather ghoulish ones out there that involved the Detroit rocker, including a persistent legend that he bit the head off a chicken and drank its blood onstage. The fowl deed supposedly took place in Toronto in 1969 during John Lennon's rather impromptu Plastic Ono concert. Cooper insists it was people in the audience who tossed chickens on stage, he simply tossed one back. Crowd members then tore into it like Col. Sanders at an herb and spice convention.

Cooper's shock rock colleague Frank Zappa apparently called him up afterwards to check out the story. When Cooper told him there was no plucking way he gave the audience the bloody bird, Zappa—himself no stranger to rumors—gave him the following advice: "Whatever you do," he told Cooper, "don't tell anyone you didn't do it." It's the old, "Don't let the truth get in the way of a good story." If fans think you might be crazy enough to do just about anything on stage, well, whatever sells tickets.

So Cooper was never in a hurry to shoot down the Eddie Haskell thing, even though—with or without rock makeup—there really was never a strong physical resemblance between the two men.

RUMOR: Ken Osmond, who played Wally's creepy pal Eddie Haskell on Leave It to Beaver, grew up to become the notorious porn star John Holmes.

FALSE: There does seem to be six degrees of separation between '50s TV teen Eddie Haskell and Alice Cooper, John Holmes, Frank Zappa, Mr. Green Jeans, and Marilyn Manson.

Unlike the Alice Cooper rumors, Leave It to Beaver star Ken Osmond really did look like John Holmes, the notorious porn star who was supposedly the biggest man in his field. The Holmes rumor was "a pain in my butt for 11 years," Osmond told TV Guide in 1998. After the series went off the air in 1963, Osmond went on to an 18-year career with the Los Angeles Police Department. Jokes about him being a porn star were an embarrassment both at work and at his church, especially when some members of his congregation began to suspect it was true.

The confusion took root, as it were, when Holmes was identified as "Eddie Haskell" on a few triple-X films by porn producers trying to cash in on the facial resemblance between the two men. Osmond tried to sue to put an end to the credit by association. The case went to the Supreme Court, where it was ruled that the use of the name was protected by satire. Osmond didn't get a penny for his troubles.

When I interviewed him a few years ago, Osmond's former costar, Tony Dow (he played Beaver's older brother, Wally), said he had heard both the

Alice Cooper and the John Holmes rumors. He'd also heard an even more embarrassing tale—when Holmes was involved in a murder investigation in the late '70s, Osmond, according to Dow, was mistakenly brought in for questioning. "He had to stand up in front of the police department and prove that he wasn't [Holmes]," said Dow. Osmond made no mention of that to *TV Guide* in 1998, but, either way, Mrs. Cleaver's frequent lament, "Ward, I'm worried about the Beaver," will never sound quite the same again.

RUMOR: *The little girl who played Tabitha on* Bewitched *grew up to become pop star Madonna.*

FALSE: *And ridiculous. First of all, which of the two Darrens was Madonna supposed to be singing to with "Pappa Don't Preach"?*

The rumor probably started when Madonna was quoted as saying she was a *Bewitched* fan growing up as a child. Or simply that "witch" rhymes with a word often associated with the pop star.

Bewitched ran from 1964 to 1972. It was about the Stevenses, Darren (Dick York and, later, Dick Sargent) and Samantha (Elizabeth Montgomery), a normal suburban couple except for one little detail—Samantha was a witch. In the second season, in 1966, they introduced a new member of the family, Tabitha. She was played not by Madonna Ciconne of Detroit, Michigan, but by twins Erin and Diane Murphy.

Interviewed in 1998, Murphy, who eventually played in most of the scenes, recalled joining the series when she was almost two.

By the time the series ended in 1972, she was eight years old. Madonna, on the other hand, would have been eight when Tabitha made her debut and far too old to play the toddler. "I worked with amazing people and the special effects were fun," remembered Murphy. "I only have positive memories." They include offscreen fun with Montgomery, who had three young kids of her own at the time. "My main memories about Liz are things we did off the set—we went trick or treating together, going to see Santa together." She recalls Montgomery and her own mother taking all the kids to the movies "and throwing popcorn at us from the balcony."

Had it been Madonna, well, you just never would have wanted to stumble across Samantha Stevens with her kids at a strip club.

CHAPTER 16

Kids Say the Darndest Things: Rumors about Children's Shows

Some of the wildest rumors and urban legends date back to the early days of television, when TV was live and, in many ways, dangerous. This was especially true with children's shows. Often hosted by newcomers to the medium, they were like experimental broadcasts, with nothing less precious than impressionable young minds at the other end of the experiment.

One non-newcomer was Art Linkletter, a smooth professional who was finding out that "kids say the darndest things" as early as 1943 on radio and continuing on television straight though until 1970. Linkletter never seemed to wear out his welcome and enjoyed one of the longest runs ever in television with *House Party* and *People Are Funny* spanning 30 years. At one point, he had shows on all three networks—ABC, CBS, and NBC—all at the same time. Linkletter basically played straight man to the kids and never spoke down to them, even though he was mainly entertaining adults, especially housewives who were predominantly the daytime viewing audience back in the '50s and into the '60s.

Other TV personalities in this chapter were mainly seen as children's entertainers, especially Soupy Sales and the Bullwinkle puppet from *Time for Beany* (memorably voiced by Bill Scott). Still, it seemed at times that they were aiming their fun over the heads of the kiddies and straight at the hipper parents in the room—or perhaps they were simply trying to amuse themselves.

RUMOR: A little boy once told Art Linkletter on the air that his daddy goes out of town on business two days a week. That's when his uncle comes over to sleep with his mommy—except he isn't really his uncle.

TRUE: When I spoke with Linkletter late in 2006, he was 94 and had just co-authored (with Chicken Soup for the Soul *series cocreator Mark Victor Hansen) his 28th book,* How to Make the Rest of Your Life the Best of Your Life.

Long before most of us were born, Linkletter made a name for himself as an affable daytime TV host. His "Kids Say the Darndest Things" segment of his daytime talk shows were extremely popular throughout the '50s and '60s. The still remarkably spry and agile TV icon was ready when I asked him about the "darndest thing" a youngster once said that basically outed his mom's infidelity.

"That happened," confirmed Linkletter. "The boy said he used to sleep with mommy—when uncle so-and-so wasn't there." That was back in the days of live TV and you got what you got, said Linkletter.

The children were saying it out of innocence," he quickly added, citing several more humorous references. He once asked a seven year old boy why he thought his teacher singled him out to be one of four children interviewed for that day's show. (Linkletter used to interview four kids a day, five days a week.) "The little boy looks up and says, 'Because I'm the smartest kid in the room.' I said, 'Did the teacher tell you that?' He says, 'No, I noticed it myself.'"

Linkletter calculates that he spoke with 27,000 children between the ages of 5 and 10 over 26 years. He once asked one of them, "Your mom and dad are always working. What do your mom and dad do for fun?" "Search me," said the child. "They always lock the door." Another time a little boy blurted that he had a secret. "My dad and mother's getting married next Tuesday." A scandalous remark in the '50s but not so much today.

RUMOR: Soupy Sales once asked kids to go into their parents' wallets and send him "those funny green pieces of paper with all those nice pictures of guys with beards on them."

TRUE: This might be the best urban legend that actually happened. The idea that some whacked out kiddie show host actually talked kids into stealing money from their parents and sending it in to a TV station sounds way too good to be true. This is, after all, the ultimate TV story, the home shopping network/televangelist/PBS pledge drive extortion stunt of all time.

Soupy Sales was the coolest of the cool kiddie show hosts. Every city had one back in the '50s and '60s. It was usually a sportscaster or weatherman picking up an extra few bucks as an on air "Uncle Bill" or "Big Al" while the station showed tired old *Popeye* or *Terry Toons*. Sales began his career in Cincinnati and Detroit, hosting local shows before breaking though nationally on ABC stations in the late '50s.

In the '60s, Sales took his act to Los Angeles where he gained notoriety tossing pies in the face of big shots like Burt Lancaster and Frank Sinatra. He was such a shameless kook, all the Rat Packers loved him. At one point, Sales was hosting a daily show in Detroit, a lunchtime program on ABC and an early evening show for KABC in Los Angeles. His shows were also syndicated to other markets throughout America. Big name Motown musical guest stars like The Supremes, Martha and the Vandellas, and The Ronettes were dropping by and risking pie attacks, as were comics like Nipsey Russell and Henny Youngman. No wonder *Howdy Doody* was chased off the air.

It was during a stint in New York at WNEW that Sales pulled his most fabled stunt. Ad libbing while filling for time on the evening of January 1, 1965, he looked straight into the camera and said, "Last night was New Year's Eve, and I bet Mommy and Daddy are real tired tonight, so tiptoe into their bedroom and get Dad's wallet or Mommy's purse and take out the little green pieces of paper that have the guys with the beards on them and send them to me here at Channel 5 in New York and I'll send you a postcard from Puerto Rico."

Sounds harmless enough, except this was 1965, and, believe it or not, kids used to do what they were told back then. According to a story in a 1998 issue of *TV Guide*, $80,000 was sent in to the station. (Although other reports suggest only a few actual dollars, plus a lot of monopoly money, was sent in.)

Sales was suspended for two weeks on charges that he was encouraging kids to steal. Today he would be made a network vice president. "It was the best thing that ever happened to me," Sales told *TV Guide*. "It made me a star."

There are several other Soupy Sales rumors that aren't true. He never went on the air and told a dirty joke which ends with the line "Every time I see 'F' you see 'K.'" That would be wrong. He got blamed for plenty other dirty jokes, including the old chestnut about the couple at the ballpark—he kissed her on the strikes and she kissed him on the balls. Hey, kids back then had to blame somebody and Soupy was a pretty popular target, as well as a noted ad libber. As Sales points out, he would have been suspended for a lot longer than two weeks if he ever said half the things he was accused of saying. Some record of those jokes would exist on some blooper record somewhere.

Unfortunately, no record exists of Sales's famous big money boo-boo. He wound up with pie or worse all over his own face when some idiot at WNEW bulk erased all those crazy tapes. Was that guy suspended for two weeks? That would be no. Nobody knew from DVD sales back then.

In the late '70s, Sales filmed a color series for KCOP in Los Angeles where he recreated many of his old routines, bringing back his puppet pals White Fang, Black Tooth, Pookie, and Hippy. Unfortunately, there was no bringing back that crazy little kiddie heist.

RUMOR: Back in the '60s, a youngster on one of those local "Bozo the Clown" kiddie shows once turned to the host and blurted, "Cram it, clown."

TRUE: And he spoke for us all. There should be a street named after this kid, perhaps a national holiday. Unfortunately we do not know his name. Perhaps he grew up to become Marilyn Manson or Al Gore. Hey, this is my book, let's start a rumor.

Bozo the Clown was the McDonald's of children's television. What that makes Ronald McDonald, I don't know—perhaps the Bozo of burger boosting.

Created to promote a series of Capitol records back in the '40s, Bozo became a TV property in the mid-50s when entrepreneur Larry Harmon bought the rights to "The World's Most Famous Clown." At this point, Emmett Kelly probably swept himself into a tiny little spotlight and died. Harmon hustled his clown concept to local stations across America.

Suddenly there were Bozos from Green Bay to Baton Rouge. But it was in Boston where Bozo really got under some kid's skin. Harmon told the story to *TV Guide* in 1998. The clown was working a live show on Boston's now defunct WCVB. It was a show Harmon happened to be producing.

It was during *Bozo's Treasure Chest*—a kiddie toy grab contest—that Junior blew his stack. Harmon says it was some "young, underprivileged kid" with "eyes as big as saucers looking at these toys" who was this close to winning a prize when he missed the third and last question. The show's ringmaster tells the kid, "You're never a loser on the Bozo show, you're just an almost-winner," and handed the kid a crummy Bozo towel. To which Junior replied, "Cram it, clown."

"That's a Bozo no-no," was apparently the clown's live and speedy response.

RUMOR: *Bill Cosby bought up the rights to* The Little Rascals *shorts to keep them off TV.*

FALSE: *Then he hid all the tapes in the Jell-O tree. Right.*

Censorship of classic films has existed for years on TV. Many of the Warner Brothers, wartime cartoons, where racial stereotypes were used to provoke laughs, are strictly verboten. You don't see Mexican rodent Speedy Gonzales talking about all those other rats after his "seester" anymore, either.

The Little Rascals, which were originally run in theatres in the '20s through the '40s under the Hal Roach "Our Gang" banner, do have instances among their 200-plus shorts that would be considered a little nonpolitically correct today. There are scenes, for example, in *Our Gang Follies of 1936*, where the black kids in the neighborhood get scared by a monkey in a ghost costume and hide in the dark—where the animated, blinking, whites of their eyes are all you can see.

With his patched clothing and pigtails, Billie "Buckwheat" Thomas makes some viewers wince today. On the other hand, he was as featured as any of the other Rascals and part of a fully integrated gang.

Thomas was also the subject of his own urban legend. When he dropped out of show business after his MGM contract expired in the early '40s, rumors spread that he was dead. For a while an imposter claimed to be the original Buckwheat, and even fooled Steve Allen's talk show and the panel series *I've Got a Secret*, getting on both shows as a guest.

Thomas finally emerged in the '70s, revealing he had been living in Los Angeles and working for a Technicolor lab.

Eddie Murphy's Buckwheat character on *Saturday Night Live*, complete with Don King fright wig and "O-tay!" expression, also added to the Buckwheat legend (and stereotype). Charges of racism have led to the delisting of other series. *Amos 'N' Andy*, wildly popular on radio in the '40s, came to TV in 1951. Pressure from the National Association for the Advancement of Colored People, whose membership found the show offensive, helped scuttle the program after just two seasons. While it lived on in syndication for a while, CBS permanently withdrew it from circulation in the wake of civil rights protests in the '60s.

By the '80s, when Bill Cosby's family sitcom, *The Cosby Show*, was by far the number one show on television, rumors began to circulate that the Cos had bought up and destroyed all the negatives to *The Little Rascals* shorts. It was well known that Cosby, sought after for years as an advertising pitchman, had become fabulously wealthy, especially after *The Cosby Show* was sold to syndication for hundreds of millions of dollars. The famous comedian was also among those who spoke out against the *Amos 'N' Andy* series. So, while he probably could have afforded to buy up the *Rascals*, he never did. King World Productions still owns the rights to the series and continues to license it, although the popularity of the series has waned in recent years.

I can recall showing a few of the original shorts on 16mm at one of my youngster's seventh or eighth birthday parties. A wave of protest went up from some of the other kids, not for any reasons of color, but that the film wasn't in color. How's that for irony.

RUMOR: Ernie and Bert are gay and will soon marry on Sesame Street.

FALSE: The folks at the Children's Television Workshop (CTW) and the Jim Henson Company who produce this multiple award-winning series are real sick of denying this one. The series' longevity—it began in the late '60s and had been a staple of PBS for more than 35 years—has probably added to the urban legend odds. Bert and Ernie are the original puppet odd couple. Ernie is a lovable slob, Bert is uptight and intense.

Muppet creator Jim Henson worked and voiced Ernie up until his death in 1990. Frank Oz performed Bert. On the show, the two pals share an apartment, sleep in the same room (although in separate beds), and enjoy playing with rubber duckies. Hey, it doesn't take much to get people talking.

An early *Saturday Night Live* "Weekend Update" report had Chevy Chase telling America that "Bert and Ernie confirmed this week that they are practicing homosexuals." *Family Guy* has also lampooned the duo, show-ing them in bed together as a bickering gay couple. Not helping may be confusion between this show and its Broadway send up, *Avenue Q*, which featured Bert and Ernie look- and sound-alikes Rod and Nicky, who were completely out of the closet. (Their big production number is titled "If You Were Gay.")

The jokes go on and on. There are rumors, always denied by CTW, that *Sesame Street* is ready to kill off one of the duo. Internet parodies over the years include a "Bert Is Evil" Web site, where he is depicted assassinating John F. Kennedy, among other atrocities.

In the '90s, *Sesame Street* did introduce a muppet to its neighborhood who was HIV-positive. Maybe they were trying to show how the series can educate and inform, not confuse and malign.

RUMOR: A Bullwinkle moose hand puppet once urged kids to glue the knobs on to their TV sets so they would be sure not to miss the show when it returned next week.

PROBABLY TRUE: Rocky and Bullwinkle were the Simpsons of their day, delighting kids, but especially their parents with jokes and references pitched right over the youngsters' heads. But one of the characters telling kids to glue the knobs on their parents' TV sets? This story always sounded a little apocryphal to me, but—like the similar Soupy Sales story about asking kids to send in dollar bills—it really did happen.

For the uninitiated, Rocky was a cheerful flying squirrel and Bullwinkle was a dumb but good-natured moose. Crudely animated, they were voiced by two of the best in the business, June Foray and Bill Scott. All the voice stars of the series were exceptional, including film and radio veterans such as William Conrad (the future *Canon* star who narrated the Bullwinkle adventures), Hans Conried (Do-Right's nemesis Snidely Whiplash), and Edward Everett Horton (who narrated the kooky *Fractured Fairy Tales*).

The witty scripts, supervised by Scott, were light years ahead of anything heard in a children's show at that time. According to one former ad agency executive I spoke with, work would stop at his place of business in the '60s when the series was on.

It probably helped that *Rocky and Bullwinkle* was produced by one of the greatest eccentrics in a field full of nut jobs, Jay Ward. He was kind of the anti-Disney, a producer of animated shows who was more interested in deconstructing fairy tales than building them up into theme parks.

Many of us remember Rocky and Bullwinkle as cartoon critters, but there was a brief but golden time in the early '60s—when the series was on NBC—when the show was introduced each week by a Bullwinkle puppet voiced and operated by Scott (also a producer on the series). *The Bullwinkle Show* opened each week with the puppet goofing on current events, celebrities of the day (such as newsmen Huntley and Brinkley), and even the famous host of the program that followed on NBC, Walt Disney. At the time, this was pretty cheeky, a bit like making fun of the Pope.

One week the moose puppet actually told viewers to yank the knobs right off their TV sets. "In that way," he said, "we'll be sure to be with you next week."

Naturally, NBC received several complaints from parents wondering what the heck was up with the talking moose. Scott tried to smooth things over. The very next week, he told kids to put those knobs back on with glue "and make it stick!" Not long after, the moose puppet was unceremoniously dropped from NBC's broadcast.

The story sounds apocryphal, but Foray, whom I spoke with in Toronto in the mid-80s, claimed that she remembered it quite clearly. Unfortunately, according to officials at The Paley Media Center in Los Angeles where I searched for this episode, only one of the Bullwinkle puppet intros survives, and it is not one of the episodes in question.

Scott, who also voiced such Jay Ward cartoon favorites as Dudley Do-Right, George of the Jungle, and Super Chicken, passed away in 1985. Ward himself didn't live much longer, but long enough for me to track him down in the mid-80s. At the time, his wife was behind the counter at the Dudley Do-Right Emporium on Sunset Boulevard, selling *Rocky and Bullwinkle* T-shirts and trinkets. When I asked about the great Jay Ward, she referred me around the corner to a cute little cottage. This was Ward's private retreat, referred to as the studio.

I walked around and knocked on the door. It eventually opened and there, unmistakable in his glasses and walrus moustache, stood Jay Ward. I told him I was a big fan and had traveled all the way from Canada. He stood there a second, said he had no idea who Jay Ward was, and slammed the door in my face.

Does that sound like the kind of a man who would put up with one of the stars of his show telling kids to glue the knobs on their parents' TV sets? Hokey smokes, it does.

CHAPTER 17

Tall 'Toon Tales: Urban Myths about Animated Series

How can there be rumors about cartoon characters? Cartoon characters can't gossip. They don't go into rehab, cheat on their wives, or hire press agents to create phony buzz. What kind of Mickey Mouse chapter idea is this?

Still, there are a number of tall 'toon tales in TV Land. They all have something to do with either the humans behind the scenes making the cartoons or the ones in front of the TV watching the cartoons.

That a couple have to do with *The Simpsons* shouldn't be surprising. *The Simpsons* isn't just the longest-running animated series ever, but the longest-running sitcom ever, surpassing *My Three Sons*, *The Danny Thomas Show*, and even *The Adventures Of Ozzie and Harriet*. It passed the 400 episode mark in 2007, during its 18th season. As Bart used to say, "Ay carumba!"

RUMOR: *Even though a pseudonym was used, Michael Jackson was the voice of a memorable character on an early episode of* The Simpsons.

TRUE: *"Yes, that was Michael Jackson,"* Simpsons *creator Matt Groening confirmed when I asked him directly at the January 2007 TV critics press tour in Los Angeles.*

For years, Groening and others denied it. In fact, executive producer James L. Brooks still refused to confirm it when I approached him at the same event as Groening. "I think we made a promise," said Brooks.

Groening later explained that keeping Jackson's contribution a secret "was a contractual thing, and I never signed the contract."

In the third-season *Simpsons* episode, "Stark Raving Dad," which first aired in September of 1991, a tubby, bald, lumpy looking character named Leon Kompowsky meets Homer in a mental institution and claims to be pop star Michael Jackson. The character sure sounds like Jackson, except at the end of the episode, when he reverts to a gruff voice more in tune with his character, which is supposed to be a New Jersey bricklayer.

Kompowsky befriends Bart and helps him write a sweet little song to his sister called, "Happy Birthday Lisa." The voice credit at the end of the episode read John Jay Smith. Go ahead, look for him on IMDb—it takes you straight to the Michael Jackson page.

Despite denials from FOX and *Simpsons'* publicists, there was immediate speculation that Jackson, always a big cartoon fan, had recorded the voice for the character. The so-called King of Pop had already earned a reputation as an eccentric, with tales of antigravity chambers and Elephant Man bone collections already making the rounds. There was, however, no whiff of child molestation accusations at the time this episode first aired.

The Simpsons had already, at this early stage, let one big name guest voice get away with hiding behind a pseudonym. In season two, Dustin Hoffman played Lisa's substitute teacher, Mr. Bergstrom. He was simply credited at the end as Sam Etic (Semitic, get it?). Word that it really was Hoffman quickly leaked out—if it wasn't already obvious in the scene where Bergstrom says, "Mrs. Krabappel, you're trying to seduce me" (a reference to Hoffman's breakout film, *The Graduate*).

In *Planet Simpson: How a Cartoon Masterpiece Documented an Era and Defined a Generation*, author Chris Turner asserts that it was indeed Jackson's voice on the episode—although only in the speaking parts, not the singing voice used on Happy Birthday Lisa (credited to voice-over actor Kip Lennon).

That is how Yeardley Smith remembers it. Smith, the voice of Lisa Simpson, recorded her lines at the same time as Jackson. "That was an extraordinary day," she recalls. She remembers Jackson as "very quiet and he was really into being there."

"It's kind of dazzling for us when you have a huge star in our environment," says Smith, who was equally starstruck when Elizabeth Taylor came in to utter baby sister Maggie's only words: "Dad-dee." Recalls Smith, "She brought her little dog with her."

The irony in all of this is that Jackson never appeared to be more flesh and blood, more human, than as cartoon character Kompowsky. The episode remains one of the most affecting *Simpsons* episodes ever.

Groening can recall only two other rumors that spread about the show, which celebrated its 400th episode in 2007. One, that Madonna was going to be a guest voice (she hasn't, so far), and the other, that the long-awaited *Simpsons* movie, released in July of 2007, was going to be about Bart losing his virginity. Groening says that rumor started years ago when somebody asked one of the *Simpsons'* writers what the eventual movie would be about. The snappy "Bart loses his virginity" answer was just a joke. D'oh!

RUMOR: A "Dear Abby" advice column was once pulled from newspapers after it was revealed that the letter was actually taken from an episode of The Simpsons.

TRUE: That sound you just heard was Nelson going, "A-Ha!"

In March of 2004, some 'toon lovin' prankster sent a bogus letter in to the long-running "Dear Abby" relationship advice column. The person, who signed her letter "Stuck in a Love Triangle," described herself as a 34-year-old woman with three children married for 10 years to a "greedy, selfish, inconsiderate and rude" husband named Gene. The woman complained that her hubby's idea of a birthday present was a bowling ball, one that had holes drilled to fit his own fingers.

The letter writer said she decided to teach the boob a lesson by striking out to the nearest bowling alley. That's where she met Franco, the man of her dreams. A relationship developed, and before you could finish a frame or pick up a spare, the woman was bowled over.

The letter to "Dear Abby" went on, stating that the woman no longer loved her husband and wanted to be with her new man, but feared her kids would be devastated. "What should I do?" she asked.

The "Dear Abby" column dates back to 1956. It was started by Pauline Phillips, who wrote under the pseudonym Abigail Van Buren. Her daughter, Jeanne Phillips, had completely taken over writing the column by the time the *Simpsons* letter crossed her desk in 2004. Not realizing it was a prank, she penned this straight down the middle of the lane response: come clean about the infidelity. "To save this marriage, he might be willing to change back to the man who bowled you over in the first place," she advised.

The letter and response were typed up and distributed by United Press Syndicate. One newspaper editor read the piece, entitled "Wife meets perfect match after husband strikes out," thought it sounded a little too familiar, and alerted the syndicate. They did some digging and—d'oh!—discovered that they'd been pranked by a *Simpsons* fan.

The letter matched the plot of one of the very first episodes of *The Simpsons*. "Life on the Fast Lane" (also known as "Jacques to Be Wild") first aired on March 18, 1990. In the episode, Homer gives Marge a bowling ball as a birthday present. She decides to teach him a lesson by striking out for the local lanes, where she almost has an affair with a handsome bowling instructor named Jacques. "Here, use my ball," purred the cad.

Fortunately, Homer got wise when he discovered a gift Jacques had given his wife—bowling gloves. The same discovery was made by the husband in the "Dear Abby" letter.

"It did sound too similar not to be a hoax," Kathie Kerr, a spokeswoman for the syndicate told the Associated Press.

Once the alert went out that the letter was stolen from an episode of *The Simpsons,* the column was spiked—or withdrawn—from circulation. Still, some newspapers chose to run with it anyway. Double d'oh!

RUMOR: *An animated cocaine reference led to the cancellation of* Mighty Mouse *in the '80s.*

FALSE: *This rumor, however, did spread like wildfire and probably led to the premature cancellation of the series. CBS revived the classic Terry Toon Mighty Mouse character in the mid-80s with a brand new Saturday Morning series called* The New Adventures of Mighty Mouse. *In a move which probably seems even more risky in hindsight, they put Ralph Bakshi—notorious for producing the triple-X cartoon feature* Fritz the Cat—*in charge of the production.*

The series was ahead of its time, hinting at the edgier gags that would later be embraced in such prime time animated adult fare as *The Simpsons, South Park,* and *The Family Guy.* In the context of the Saturday morning kiddie zone and the stifling, politically correct atmosphere of the "Just say no" Reagan era, however, the show was watched like a hawk by pressure groups.

So when Mighty Mouse sniffed a flower, inhaled some white dust, and seemed to gain a burst of energy, the CBS switchboard lit up. CBS dropped the show even after the animators insisted it was just an innocent gag. "Ridiculous," says supervising animator John Kricfalusi, whom I spoke with in 2001. "That scene was so innocent. Especially when you consider that there were so many other things they could have gotten us on." Now there's a defense.

RUMOR: *The title of the Hanna-Barbera hit* Scooby-Doo, Where Are You? *came from a Frank Sinatra song.*

TRUE: *Ol' Blue Eyes probably had no idea he crooned cartoon powerhouse Hanna-Barbera into a gold mine. The TV cartoon factory, which had cranked out such hits as* The Flintstones, The Jetsons, *and* The Adventures of Jonny Quest *in the early '60s, were looking for their next Saturday morning hit. As he recounts in his 1994 biography,* My Life in 'Toons, *producer Joe Barbera had pitched a new series to CBS about a group of teenagers and a dog mixed up in a series of supernatural adventures. Network boss Fred Silverman liked the concept, but wasn't crazy about the titles being suggested, including* I'm S-s-s-s-scared *and* Mysteries Five.

Silverman was flying home to Los Angeles from the meeting in New York and started listening to a music station on the airline earphones. On came the Sinatra hit, "Strangers in the Night," with Sinatra's infectious little warble, "Scooby-dooby-doo..."

As Barbera, who passed away in 2006 at 95, tells it, Silverman arrived late that night for a meeting with the cartoon executives and announced he had the title: *Scooby-Doo, Where Are You?* Barbera yelled, "Terrific!" and handed Silverman a Tanqueray martini. "Actually," added Barbera, "at that hour he could have said anything and I would have responded in much the same way."

Silverman knew a good title when he heard one: *Scooby-Doo* lasted seven seasons and inspired several spin-offs.

RUMOR: A 1997 episode of Pokemon *triggered epileptic seizures in more than 600 young viewers.*

PARTLY TRUE: This sounds like one that parents started. Ever since the Japanese cartoon series became a monster hit in 1999, parents have been searching for any excuse to banish it from the airwaves. There have been several reports that 618 Japanese children experienced seizures from viewing an episode of the original series, Pocket Monsters, *in 1997.*

The problem stemmed from a pulsing burst of light and color. Those scenes were immediately edited out of the series in Japan and never aired in North America, despite the show's hypnotic pull on youngsters here. The *Southern Medical Journal* followed up and apparently found that only a small fraction of the 618 children actually suffered from photosensitive epilepsy. Many more parents suffered from photosensitive bankruptcy.

CHAPTER 18

Strikes, Spares, and Misses: TV's Most Enduring Sports Myths

Think there aren't any tall tales in the world of TV sports? Think again. You've probably heard for years that the "halftime flush" at the annual Super Bowl broadcast pushes water systems to the brink in cities all across America. Or that more clothing is stained on Super Bowl Sunday than at any other day of the year. Or that Disneyland and Walt Disney World are deserted each year on the day of the big Super Bowl broadcast.

All good stories, but, like much about the Super Bowl, more hype than reality.

Fact is, there is no real proof that public water systems are tested to the max during the halftime of a Super Bowl broadcast. When the Chicago Bears went to the 2007 Super Bowl, a reporter at the *Chicago Tribune* checked with the Windy City's Department of Water Management. A spokesman there said the utility was prepared for a "slight fluctuation at halftime," but nothing the system couldn't handle.

Besides, who wants to miss the halftime show? Somebody could be randomly ripping off Janet Jackson's clothes.

Ex-Bears coach and TV commentator Mike Ditka is partially responsible for perpetuating this full-flushed fabrication. The coach once shot a TV ad for Scott brand toilet paper where he barked at folks to "get out there and fight the halftime flush."

There's no denying that the Super Bowl is an enormous TV draw. Super Bowl XLI, the soggy 2007 tilt between the Indianapolis Colts and the Bears, drew an average audience of 93.2 million viewers, peaking at close to 100 million around halftime. CBS estimates that 139.77 million U.S. viewers watched at least part of the game. That ranks it as the second-highest-rated Super Bowl ever and the third most watched TV show of all time, behind only Super Bowl XXX in 1996 and the 1983 *M*A*S*H* finale.

In this age of rapidly expanding new media alternatives and audience fragmentation, nothing comes even remotely close to that size of a TV audience. Yet there are still 170 million Americans who don't watch a second of the Super Bowl, and several thousand of them are at Disney World, just as they are on any other day.

As for the Super Bowl stained shirt rumor, well, I'm still waiting for all those dry cleaners to get back to me.

RUMOR: *The first two Super Bowls have been lost to posterity, as the networks erased the original tapes.*

TRUE: *As in, sad but true. Today, when content is king and even the most banal TV product is repackaged and remarketed again and again, it is almost impossible to believe somebody erased the first two NFL-AFL Championship game tapes. I mean, c'mon, you can get all six seasons of* Hogan's Heroes *on DVD but not Super Bowls I and II??*

Then again, this was 1967 and 1968. Home VCRs were a thing of the future. The Super Bowl wasn't even called the Super Bowl back then, it was referred to as the AFL-NFL World Championship Game.

The nickname Super Bowl was already being used, however; and, yes, that rumor is also true—the name was inspired by those dark purple hard rubber "super balls" that were so popular in school yards in the '60s. Lamar Hunt, the Kansas City Chiefs owner who died in December of 2006, is credited with coining the term "Super Bowl" after watching his kids play with those high-bouncing Wham-O creations.

Hunt's Chiefs were in that first Super Bowl against the Green Bay Packers. Played on January 15, 1967, the Packers, led by quarterback Bart Starr and legendary coach Vince Lombardi, won easily with a score of 35 to 10.

It was the only Super Bowl game broadcast by two major U.S. networks, CBS, which had national rights to NFL games, and NBC, which had the AFL rights. Did that help prevent one of those networks from erasing the tape of the game? It did not.

Announcers Ray Scott, Jack Whitaker, and Frank Gifford worked the CBS booth while Curt Gowdy and Paul Christman called the game for NBC. That's what we're told, anyway, since there is no proof.

One interesting sidenote: due to an extended commercial break, NBC missed the kickoff at the start of the second half. Field officials actually stopped the game and had the kickoff restarted once NBC was back on the air. Even then, TV was calling the shots. Too bad nobody thought to save the tapes.

The network even split the postgame show, with CBS's Pat Summerall and NBC's George Ratterman sharing one mike as trophies were presented. Also lost to posterity was the halftime show, which featured trumpeter Al Hirt and the University of Arizona and the University of Michigan marching bands. Future generations will never know for sure if there were any Janet Jackson-like wardrobe malfunctions.

A small part of the original Super Bowl broadcast, featuring Green Bay wide receiver Max McGee's opening touchdown, has surfaced. The Paley Media Center (formerly The Museum of Television and Radio) has put out the call to hobbyists and archivists in the hope that any further record of this game or the second lost Super Bowl broadcast might some day turn up. Among the many other "lost" broadcasts on the Center's wish list are Don Larsen's perfect game in the 1956 World Series, the first televised address from the White House (in 1947, by Harry S. Truman) and 14 TV appearances by James Dean.

Super Bowl III—in which Joe Namath's New York Jets upset the favored Baltimore Colts—is the first Super Bowl broadcast preserved in its entirety.

RUMOR: *Baseball commentator Dizzy Dean once got away with a dirty joke in the middle of a game.*

UNSUBSTANTIATED: *Here's the story. During a CBS baseball broadcast, a camera pans over to a pair of lovers in the stands. Pee Wee Reese and Dizzy Dean are in the booth. "Look at that, Pee Wee," says Dean. "He kisses her on the strikes and she kisses him on the balls."*

Jerome Hanna "Dizzy" Dean was a major league pitcher for the St. Louis Cardinals (where he was known as the ace of the "Gashouse Gang") and the Chicago Cubs throughout the '30s and into the '40s. His career cut short due to injury, he became a broadcaster and was famous for his fractured, Southern sayings.

Among the things that he really did say: "The Good Lord was good to me. He gave me a strong right arm, a good body, and a weak mind," and, "Don't fail to miss tomorrow's game!"

So the idea that Dean and only Dean could have gotten away with such a silly sexual innuendo during a live sports broadcast fits perfectly with his dizzy persona.

Dean, however, died in 1974, and there is no record of his ever addressing the "kissing him on the balls" legend. Others have dismissed it as apocryphal, including NBC play-by-play announcer Bob Costas.

Usually incidents that sound too much like jokes turn out to be just that—jokes. The "balls" reference turns up time and again, whether it is baseball, tennis or golf. The long-standing rumor that Johnny Carson once asked Arnold Palmer's wife if she did anything for good luck before a tournament—like kiss his balls (see chapter 1)—also turned out to be just an old joke tucked into a *Tonight Show* setting. You can almost hear Carson or Dean say these things, which helps convince people they really did.

Also adding to the legends is the lack of refutable evidence. As with all those early episodes of *The Tonight Show*, so many early baseball broadcasts are lost. Broadcasters routinely taped over early TV sports events, convinced nobody would be interested in looking at them later once they knew the score.

Still, Dizzy Dean said a lot of crazy things during baseball broadcasts. Harold Henry "Pee Wee" Reese, an all-star shortstop with the Brooklyn and Los Angeles Dodgers in the '40s and '50s, was a play-by-play announcer with Dean on CBS from 1960 to 1965. In a 1998 *TV Guide* article, Reese's son, Mark, said he asked his father about the infamous on-air rumor. "He said he didn't remember it," said the younger Reese, although his dad said it could have happened.

In the same article, Reese's brother-in-law, Bob Walton, said he swore he heard Dean make the crack, but not opposite Reese. Walton claims he heard it back when Dean was paired with his original on-air partner, Buddy Blattner. Blattner and Dean were teamed in the CBS booth from 1955 to 1959.

Blattner himself said he didn't remember the exchange taking place during the "Game of the Week" broadcasts he shared with Dean. "Listen," Blattner told *TV Guide*, "Diz did some things that I will long remember and are not to be repeated, but that's one I would have taken notice of."

RUMOR: Howard Cosell once got drunk on the air during a broadcast of Monday Night Football.

TRUE: Cosell, the "mouth that roared," was first teamed on Monday Night Football *with play-by-play man Keith Jackson (former New York Giants quarterback Frank Gifford, still under contract to CBS, arrived later) and "Dandy" Don Meredith*

at the start of the 1970 season. The trio was an instant success, with Monday
Night Football *finishing the 1970 to 1971 season as TV's third-highest rated new
program. The series became one of the most successful and enduring TV programs
ever, a top-10 hit even as it left ABC at the end of the 2005 to 2006 season and
headed to ABC's ESPN sports network.*

Still, back in the fall of 1970, America still wasn't quite sure what to make
of the lawyer turned sports announcer who made a name for himself cover-
ing the dramatic ring career of heavyweight champion Muhammad Ali. Did
they love him or hate him? Did he belong in a football booth even though,
as critics charged, "He never played the game?" Polls put him at the top of
the most-loved and most-hated sportscaster lists. His nasally, know-it-all
drone and "tell it like it is" style grated on many viewers.

Roone Arledge, the visionary ABC Sports executive who gambled that
Cosell could elevate *Monday Night Football* beyond its usual football follow-
ing, stuck by Cosell, even when powerful sponsors such as the Ford Motor
Company complained that he was a distraction to the game.

There did seem to be genuine friction in the booth between Cosell, the
New York egghead intellectual, and Meredith, folksy country charmer and
former Dallas Cowboys quarterback turned broadcaster. Still, audiences
seemed to love the banter and jabs almost as much as the football.

"Isn't Fair Hooker a great name?" Meredith asked his booth mates that very
first *Monday Night Football* game when the Cleveland wide receiver caught a
pass. Jackson "passed" and Cosell, for once, sat silent. "Fair Hooker," said
Meredith. "I haven't met one yet."

The chemistry in the booth was tested on the night of November 23,
1970, when *Monday Night Football* traveled to Philadelphia for a game
between the Eagles and the New York Giants. Cosell, who hadn't been feeling great, attended a pregame promotional party where he reportedly drank
to excess. Later that night during the broadcast, he could be heard slurring
his words, at halftime referring to the Eagles as from "Phuldulpha." This
was after he had thrown up all over Meredith's cowboy boots.

Cosell left after halftime, getting into a cab for the $92 cab ride back to
Manhattan. He later claimed he had been suffering from "toxic vertigo," an
inner ear infection that can sometimes cause loss of balance and thickness
of speech. Arledge stood by Cosell, said his star booth man had one drink
before the game and waited for the press furor to die down, which it did.

Further tales of *Monday Night Football* imbibing were woven into *Monday
Night Mayhem*, a book and later an entertaining TNT cable movie starring
John Turturro as Cosell.

Cosell remained with *Monday Night Football* until his abrupt departure before the 1984 season, when he suggested that the NFL had become "a stagnant bore." His bitter memoir, *I Never Played the Game*, published in 1985, further estranged him from his former ABC colleagues; he passed away in 1995.

RUMOR: The skier who tumbles down the hill during the "agony of defeat" segment of ABC's Wide World of Sports *died as a result of that accident.*

FALSE: Millions of Americans can recite host Jim McKay's dramatic opening to Wide World of Sports *by heart:*

> Spanning the globe to bring you the constant variety of sport! The thrill of victory...and the agony of defeat! The human drama of athletic competition! This is ABC's Wide World of Sports!

The guy who came to be known as "Mr. Agony of Defeat" was none other than Vinko Bogataj, a respected Slovene ski jumper whose nasty spill was rerun over that famous phrase every Saturday afternoon throughout the '70s and '80s and into the '90s on the introduction to the popular ABC Sports program.

The event where the spill took place was the 1970 World Ski Flying Championships, held in Oberstdorf, West Germany, on March 21, 1970. Bogataj was competing for Yugoslavia at the time.

As ABC cameras recorded, heavy snow had made the ramp a little too fast. Bogataj tried to make a correction on the way down, but instead lost his balance and completely flipped off the end of the ramp, his arms and legs flailing wildly as he tumbled and flipped through the air, eventually crashing through a small retaining fence.

The good news was the Bogataj, who spent a night in the hospital, suffered only a mild concussion and bruises. He competed again, but never with the same daring or success.

Years later, McKay told NBC's Bob Costas that Bogataj was invited to the United States to attend a couple of anniversary dinners for *Wide World of Sports*. At one dinner, recalled McKay, Bogataj "and the Olympic hockey team were the only people to get standing ovations."

The former athlete still lives in his home town of Lesce, Slovenia—where *Wide World of Sports* never aired. Bogataj, said McKay, "Had no clue why he was famous over here—he's not famous in Yugoslavia."

One ironic side note: in 2002, Bogataj got into a minor car accident in a hotel parking lot on his way to be interviewed about his famous crash by ABC's Terry Gannon. Said Bogataj, "Every time I'm on ABC, I crash."

RUMOR: In 2003, CNN reported that former Los Angeles Laker star Earvin "Magic" Johnson was near death and in a coma.

FALSE: CNN never reported any such thing. The Internet hoax, which first surfaced late in 2003, was likely perpetrated by some Internet doofus who simply plugged Johnson's name into a 1996 report about the health of convicted Martin Luther King assassin James Earl Ray.

The phony e-mail cited CNN as the source and took quotes from the Ray article—"His eyes are open, but it's just a dead stare. He could go any day now"—and applied them to the made up story about Johnson.

Ray died in prison in 1998 at the age of 70. Johnson was in good health in 2007, despite acknowledging on November 7, 1991, that he had tested HIV-positive. He immediately retired from the Lakers, although he came out of retirement on several occasions, once to join the U.S. gold medal–winning "Dream Team" at the 1992 Olympics.

CHAPTER 19

This Just In: Urban Myths about Newscasts

D id you ever wonder if Andy Rooney really did put down the French like they said he did in that Internet e-mail? And what about the time he goofed on Monica Lewinsky? Or the 20 other questionable remarks he supposedly made in that raving mad e-mail?

Seems that, if you want to sell your joke on the Internet, attach a legitimate news name to it. Andy Rooney's name is good—the curmudgeonly *60 Minutes* commentator is known for popping off on just about any subject, or at least that is how he is often parodied on *Saturday Night Live* or *Mad TV*.

But just about any well-known news personality will do. Barbara Walters, Diane Sawyer, Dan Rather, Tom Brokaw, even Walter Cronkite. Seems like you're not a real news anchor in America until you've had a nutty rumor attached to your name.

Then there are all those local news people—but the list goes on and on. It would appear that, especially in this age of *The Onion*, *The Daily Show*, and other news parodies, everyone wants to be in on the news, even when the news is faked.

RUMOR: *Andy Rooney once said on* 60 Minutes *that the French have not earned the right to protest against the United States.*

TRUE: *Rooney's acerbic "A Few Minutes with . . ." commentaries, which for decades have come at the end of the popular CBS Sunday night news magazine, are the stuff of legend. While most of his observations dealt with everyday things like the price of gas or annoying relatives, there were nights when Rooney would tackle serious issues with all the wit and candor of a raging granddaddy.*

Eventually, like Groucho Marx or even comedian George Carlin after him, just about anything politically or socially outrageous anybody said was being attributed to Andy Rooney.

This is especially true on the Internet, where—to his great annoyance—various bogus Rooney rumors have circulated for years. They typically take the form of anonymous e-mails which purport to contain the text of one of his TV rants. In the more unfortunate examples, there is a racist or sexually intolerant message in the text. (See the false Rooney rumor that follows in this chapter.)

What makes these rumors seem slightly plausible is the fact that Rooney, who kept at his *60 Minutes* gig well into his 80s, is famous for being cranky and curmudgeonly. Now and then he will actually say something with all the sting of the false stories that are being circulated. A good example is this anti-French rant, delivered by Rooney on *60 Minutes* on February 16, 2003.

With feelings against the French government running high in the wake of that nation's stand against the U.S. invasion of Iraq, Rooney didn't mince words. "You can't beat the French when it comes to food, fashion, or wine," he began, "but they lost their licence to have an opinion on world affairs years ago. They may even be selling stuff to Iraq and don't want to hurt business. The French are simply not reliable partners in a world where the good people in it ought to be working together.

"Americans may come off as international jerks sometimes," Rooney continued, "but we're usually trying to do the right thing. The French lost World War II to the Germans in about 20 minutes."

Rooney went on to say that "the French have not earned their right to oppose President Bush's plans to attack Iraq. On the other hand, I have." He briefly served as an artilleryman during World War II and was later, as an Army combat journalist for the military newspaper *Stars and Stripes*, reassigned to cover many of that war's epic battles, including the allied invasion of Normandy.

Rooney complained that the French now seemed embarrassed about their war record and didn't want to call attention to the fact that they were freed from occupation by the Brits, Canadians, and Americans. "I heard Steven Spielberg say the French wouldn't even let him film the D-Day scenes in *Saving Private Ryan* on the Normandy beaches," Rooney continued. "They want people to forget the price we paid getting their country back for them.

"I went into Paris with American troops the day we liberated it," Rooney went on to state in his commentary. "It was one of the great days in the history of the world."

Nowadays, when he drives around the Place de la Concorde, and "some French driver blows his horn at me," said Rooney, "I just smile. I say to myself, 'Go ahead, Pierre. Be my guest. I know something about this very place you'll never know.'"

RUMOR: Andy Rooney once said the following on 60 Minutes: *"Monica Lewinsky turned 28 this week. It seems like only yesterday that she was crawling around the White House on her hands and knees."*

FALSE: In the first place, it sounds more like a David Letterman or Jay Leno joke. But for some reason, people get these e-mails with jabs attributed to Rooney and are quick to believe that they were uttered by the popular CBS commentator.

Rooney, for one, doesn't think they're funny. In October of 2005, responding to a widely circulated e-mail purporting to be a *60 Minutes* transcript, he tried to set the record straight. "There's a collection of racist and sexist remarks on the Internet under a picture of me with the caption, 'Andy Rooney Said on *60 Minutes*,'" he told his audience. "If I could find the person who did write it using my name I would sue him."

No one knows who started or circulated the false *60 Minutes* e-mail but many of the jokier comments, as traced by the sleuths at the Snopes's Urban Legend Reference Pages, came from comedian Sean Morey. In some cases, a whole routine performed by Morey on *The Tonight Show* seems to have been lifted and attributed to Rooney.

One of Morey's jokes in the Rooney e-mail goes like this: "My grandmother has a bumper sticker on her car that says, 'Sexy Senior Citizen.' You don't want to think of your grandmother that way, do you? Out entering wet shawl contests. Makes you wonder where she got that dollar she gave you for your birthday."

Another one went: "Have you ever noticed that they put advertisements in with your bills now? I get back at them. I put garbage in with my check when I mail it in. I write, 'Could you throw this away for me? Thank you.'"

While these jokes really don't harm his reputation, Rooney was more incensed at another bogus e-mail that claimed to represent his political views. This e-mail, which circulated in 2003, had Rooney sounding like a racist, homophobic redneck, sounding off on everything from the United Negro College Fund to the Boy Scouts of America. "If you want to be an

American citizen you should have to speak English!" was one of the least offensive lines in the bogus commentary.

Rooney denounced the e-mail and defended his reputation in a 2003 *60 Minutes* appearance. "Hundreds of people have written asking if I really wrote the 20 detestable remarks made under my name that have had such a wide circulation on the Internet," he said. "Some of the remarks, which I will not repeat here, are viciously racist and the spirit of the whole thing is nasty, mean and totally inconsistent with my philosophy of life. It is apparent that the list of comments has been read by hundreds of thousands of Americans, many of whom must believe that it accurately represents opinions of mine that I don't dare express in my column or on television. It is seriously damaging to my reputation."

So, if you ever wondered if Andy Rooney really said all those nasty things in that e-mail, he didn't.

Part of the problem, too, is that Rooney has been spoofed so many times on TV, especially on shows like *Saturday Night Live*, that the line between reality and parody has been blurred. It's like how millions remember hearing Jack Webb utter, "Just the facts, ma'am," over and over again on *Dragnet*, even though Webb never said that line—humorist Stan Freberg did in a popular *Dragnet* parody.

Another false e-mail had Rooney going on and on in praise of older women. A typical passage: "A woman over 40 will never wake you in the middle of the night to ask, 'What are you thinking?' She doesn't care what you think."

Again, it sounds cranky enough to be plausible, although further passages were a little more saccharine. "Older women are generous with praise," it continued. "They know what it's like to be unappreciated."

The e-mail was in fact drawn from an article penned in 2000 by Frank Kaiser, a syndicated, Florida-based columnist who has been heralded as "the Andy Rooney of the Internet." Kaiser, a retired ad man, runs his own Web site (suddenlysenior.com). In 2002, he received one of the false e-mails and spotted his work attributed to Rooney. He contacted the CBS newsman, who called back, but was less than thrilled about the mix up. "He's just as cantankerous on the phone as he is on the air," Kaiser told Susan Reimer of the *Milwaukee Journal Sentinel*.

Reimer also spoke with Rooney, who told her that he was sick and tired of all these phony e-mails and that he was exploring legal action. "It just bugs me," he said, "that anybody would put my name on something I didn't write."

Asked finally if he shared Kaiser's affection for older women, Rooney stayed completely in character. His response? "Not particularly."

RUMOR: In order to cover up an extramarital affair, CBS News anchor Dan Rather made up a story about being attacked by a crazy man who kept asking, "What's the frequency, Kenneth?"

FALSE: As Dan Rather would say, this rumor "swept through the south like a tornado through a trailer park."

The controversial Texan, who served as a network news anchor longer than anyone else on American TV (from 1981 to 2005), became known almost as much for being in the news as he was for reporting it. The CBS newsman wasn't as out there as Howard Beale, the "mad prophet of the airwaves" from Paddy Chayefsky's brilliant 1976 satire, *Network*, but as the years went on, he made Beale seem less mad and more of a prophet.

There was the time in 1968 on live TV that Rather was bullied off the floor of the Democratic National convention. The time he got in a heated, on-air argument with then Vice President George H. Bush. The six minutes of dead air in 1987 when a tennis match threatened to cut into his newscast. The week in 1986 he signed off his newscast with the phrase, "Courage."

And, most famous of all, the time he got mugged by a stranger who kept repeating the same odd phrase: "Kenneth, what's the frequency?"

Rather was walking along Park Avenue in Manhattan around 11 P.M. on October 4, 1986—returning home from dinner at a friend's house—when he was attacked. (Rather told police there were two men, but only one actually attacked him.) Things got pretty rough as Rather was punched and kicked; he eventually fled to a hotel lobby to get out of harm's way.

According to Rather and other eyewitnesses at the time, including the doorman and building supervisor at the hotel, the assailants kept taunting Rather with the kooky "frequency" phrase, addressing him as Kenneth.

Three nights later, on the CBS news, the embattled newsman stuck to his story. "I got mugged," he said. "Who understands these things? I didn't and I don't now. I didn't make a lot of it at the time and I don't now. I wish I knew who did it and why, but I have no idea."

It would be years before anybody did. In the wake of the incident, rumors spread. Rather was attacked by a jealous husband after an extramarital affair. (He has been married to his wife Jean since 1957.) Rather was attacked by a KGB agent. Rather was attacked by Walter Cronkite (okay, I just made that last one up).

The tale even inspired the 1994 R.E.M. hit "What's the Frequency, Kenneth?" Lead singer Michael Stipe called the bizarre incident "the premier unsolved American surrealist act of the twentieth century." Even more bizarre was the sight of Rather "helping" Stipe and R.E.M. perform the song during a sound check at Madison Square Garden in 1995; the clip was shown the next night on *The Late Show with David Letterman*.

In 1997, 11 years after the attack, a TV critic for the *New York Daily News* claimed he knew who attacked Rather. The alleged assailant, William Tager, was identified in a photo with the article. Rather took one look at the shot and agreed that it looked like the man who attacked him in 1986.

Rather may have been incredibly fortunate. On August 31, 1994, Tager somehow was able to sneak an assault rifle to the midtown Manhattan set of NBC's *The Today Show*. NBC technician Cambell Montgomery spotted the gun and pointed Tager out to the police, but not before he was gunned down. It all took place just blocks from the Rather incident.

Regarded as mentally unhinged, Tager was interviewed by psychiatrist Park Dietz to see if he was fit to stand trial. Tager told Dr. Dietz that he killed the stagehand because the news media was beaming signals into his head and he needed to change the frequency. After examining the similarities, Dietz concluded that there was "no question" that, years earlier, it was Tager who assaulted Rather. He relayed his findings to the *Daily News*, solving the decade-long crime.

After confessing to the murder of Montgomery, Tager was sentenced to 25 years in prison in 1996. Tager, however, was never charged in the assault on Rather.

The story, strangely, doesn't end there. In a December 2001 article in *Harper's Bazaar* titled, "The Frequency," Paul Allman makes a bizarre literary assertion. It turns out that there is a character named Kenneth who runs through several short stories by the "father of postmodern fiction," Donald Barthelme—a man who was born the same year as Rather (1931) and grew up in the same town (Houston, Texas). In one of Barthelme's stories where Kenneth appears, "Kierkegaard Unfair to Schlegel" (from the 1981 collection, *Sixty Stories*) the phrase, "What is the frequency?" is used. Another Barthelme story mentions a lecherous editor named "Lather." There are also references to both CBS and *60 Minutes*.

Allman's outrageous premise is that it wasn't Tager who roughed up Rather that night, it was Barthelme, who ordered a hit on his apparent hometown rival. Allman even translated his theory into a 2004 play, titled— you guessed it—"What's The Frequency, Kenneth?"

To which we only have one word of advice for Dan Rather: "Courage."

RUMOR: Former U.S. president Lyndon Johnson used to phone CBS news anchor Walter Cronkite during the nightly newscast if he didn't like what was being said on the air.

TRUE: Cronkite himself confirmed this to a room full of reporters at a January 2006, Television Critics Association press tour session.

"He would jump up apparently and grab the phone after I'd done something he didn't like on the air, and he'd call and insist on talking to me," Cronkite, then 89, said of the former president. "I was on the air. He could see me right there. And the poor secretary there who picked up the phone when we were on the air from my office right off the newsroom would say, 'Well, he's on the air, Mr. President.' 'Goddamn it, I know he's on the air,'" said Cronkite, imitating Johnson. "'Get him on there.'"

The nightly newscasts were a big hit at the Johnson White House. A seven-eighths scale replica of the Oval Office at the Lyndon Baines Johnson (LBJ) Library and Museum in Austin, Texas, shows a console containing three large TV monitors facing Johnson's favorite chair. From there Johnson could watch all three newscasts at the same time, adjusting the sound from a large panel of buttons beside his chair. Cronkite and other news offenders were always only a phone call away.

When that call came through, recalled Cronkite, a CBS secretary would have to put up with Johnson "shouting until I was actually off the air. And then he'd get through to me and demand some kind of retraction of a story we'd just done. He felt that he could control those things. He quite obviously didn't with any news organization that I know of."

By the end of his presidency, there was little Cronkite was reporting—especially in his coverage of the Vietnam War—that Johnson wanted to hear. This was never more true than on the night of February 27, 1968, when Cronkite delivered an editorial in the wake of the Tet Offensive that was devastating to the president. It followed a trip the newsman took to Vietnam to see firsthand how the U.S. military was doing in that region. "To say that we are closer to victory today is to believe in the face of the evidence the optimists who have been wrong in the past," Cronkite began. He went on to say that "it is increasingly clear to this reporter that the only rational way out then would be to negotiate, not as victors, but as an honorable people who lived up to their pledge to defend democracy and did the best they could."

Here was "the most trusted man in America," TV's "Uncle Walter," saying it was time to get out of Vietnam.

Yep, said Cronkite, the phone rang after that broadcast. Johnson was incensed that Cronkite had basically declared the war unwinnable. "If I've lost Walter Cronkite, I've lost Middle America," is what Johnson is reported to have said following that newscast.

About a month later, on March 31, 1968, Johnson went on national television, offered a cease-fire, and then, to the shock of many viewers, dropped out of the 1968 presidential race.

"To my mind, there was no doubt that he had already made that decision," Cronkite said of his role in Johnson's downfall. "My piece just kind of was a another bullet in his rear end."

Cronkite did speak about the incident later with Johnson, who died in 1973. The outgoing president sat with the CBS newsman for an exit interview, conducted at the LBJ ranch in Texas. "I spent some time down on the ranch doing the piece, and he was quite friendly," said Cronkite. "He put all the blame on the war, of course, on the Pentagon and the military followers. He wouldn't take any blame for it himself. That was, I think, not unusual for his attitude about things."

RUMOR: 20/20 host Barbara Walters once asked an Afghani woman why she still observed the custom of walking five paces behind her husband. "Land mines," the woman replied.

FALSE: Let's face it—this is just an old joke that has been revived in the Internet age and has circulated as an e-mail. The Barbara Walters version, sometimes referring to women from Kuwait, began to appear as early as 2001. In truth, no such interview or conversation ever took place. The e-mail usually ends with the line, "The moral of the story—behind every man is a smart woman."

Another version of the story goes that the women now walk 5 or 10 paces in front of their husbands. Walters thinks this is progress and then gets hit with the "land mines" punch line again.

The joke was told in the Vietnam War era about land mines in that country and even dates back to World War II.

For Walters, the issue of land mines is no joke. In separate interviews with the likes of Princess Diana and Heather Mills, she spoke about the more than 60 million land mines buried throughout the world.

RUMOR: A local newscaster once shot herself on the air to illustrate a story about suicide.

TRUE: Would that this one were false.

Christine Chubbuck hosted a morning community affairs news magazine, Suncoast Digest, which followed the PTL Club on Sarasota, Florida's WXLT (now WWSB). At 9:30 A.M. on the morning of July 15, 1974, Chubbuck launched into what she told her crew was going to be a recap of the previous day's headlines.

Although a little unusual (Chubbuck usually opened the show with lighthearted banter and had guests waiting in the studio), the segment started well. Chubbuck ran through three national stories smoothly. Then came a technical snafu during a report on a shooting that had occurred the previous day at the local Beef and Bottle restaurant near the Sarasota-Bradenton airport. The 16mm film clip jammed in the projector and wouldn't roll.

Chubbuck, who could get a little edgy when things went wrong, according to coworkers, seemed to shrug this one off. Then she looked into the camera and told her unsuspecting audience, "In keeping with Channel 40's policy of bringing you the latest in blood and guts, and in living color, you are going to see another first: an attempted suicide."

Chubbuck then drew a .38 caliber revolver out of the bag of puppets she had placed beneath her desk and shot herself behind her right ear.

As documented in a story by Sally Quinn, published a month later in the *Washington Post*, Chubbuck's long brown hair "flew up around her face as though a sudden gust of wind had caught it." She fell violently forward, slipping completely out of camera range.

At first, camerawoman Jean Reed thought it was some kind of a sick joke. As Chubbuck's body started to twitch, however, the full horror of what had just taken place sunk in for Reed.

The station quickly faded to black, switched to a public service spot, and then ran a movie. By this time, the switchboard had lit up with calls to the station from horrified viewers asking if Chubbuck was really shot.

She was, and her self-inflicted wound proved fatal. The 29-year-old was rushed to Sarasota Memorial Hospital (a place where she often volunteered, entertaining developmentally disabled children with homemade puppets) and was pronounced dead 14 hours after the on-air shooting.

In one of several chilling twists, Chubbuck left behind a blood-soaked news story, written in longhand, detailing her suicide attempt and predicting she would be declared dead 11 hours later. When her death was officially announced, a statement she had prepared in advance was released by WXLT.

Family members and coworkers described Chubbuck as respected but troubled. She used to joke about her dead-end romantic life (she had formed a group called The Dateless Wonders Club in college) and how she had never had a serious relationship. "She'd walk into a room and every head would turn," said her mother after the funeral, "yet nobody ever asked for her phone number."

A flirtation with a coworker had been rejected. She was depressed, especially after an operation to remove an ovary cast doubt on her ability to conceive.

Shortly before her sudden death, she had clashed with the station owner and news director over Channel 40's fixation with "blood and guts" on the news. The same month she died, she quizzed local police officers about the surest way to commit suicide, suggesting she was researching a news story. She had even grimly joked with one coworker about taking her own life on the air.

Thomas Beacon, the Presbyterian minister who delivered the eulogy at her funeral, summed it all up: "We suffer at our sense of loss, we are frightened by her rage, we are guilty in the face of her rejection, we are hurt by her choice of isolation, and we are confused by her message."

The two-inch master tape of Chubbock's final minutes was seized by the local sheriff's department and eventually released to the family. Mercifully, it looks like it has not survived into the age of YouTube.

CHAPTER 20

Miscellaneous Myths: Items That Simply Defy Categorization

What goes together better than awards shows and *Entertainment Tonight*? Okay, several things, but these two rumors just don't seem to fit in any other categories, so here they are, lumped together for your reading pleasure.

It's not that there aren't several good stories about things that went on at awards shows over the years. Like the fact that Jayne Mansfield exhaled a little too vigorously at the 1956 Academy Awards, thrusting one of her ample breasts into living rooms all across America. Somehow, the world did not end; that would happen decades later when Janet Jackson wrecked the Super Bowl by doing something memorable.

Still, that was never an award show rumor. Here is one that was, plus a follow up from *Entertainment Tonight*.

RUMOR: Marisa Tomei won the 1992 Academy Award for Best Supporting Actress because Oscar presenter Jack Palance read her name by mistake.

FALSE: Whoever started this rumor should be forced to do 100 one-armed push ups. Gossip about Tomei's undeserved Oscar win started to spread shortly after the 1993 award ceremony. That was the Oscar telecast where host Billy Crystal kept goofing on his City Slickers *costar Jack Palance.*

The veteran actor, whose career dated back to memorable roles in westerns such as *Shane* (1953), sent up his own tough guy image in *City Slickers*.

He won his own Best Supporting Actor Academy Award as cowboy Curly Washburn in the 1991 comedy.

Ambling up to accept the award, the imposing, six foot four actor snarled down at host Crystal and repeated one of the crowd-pleasing lines from the comedy—"I crap bigger than him." Then, to demonstrate his fitness level, the 73-year-old proceeded to hit the deck of the award show stage to do several one-handed push ups. "That's nothing, really, Palance said after. "As far as two-handed push ups, you can do that all night and it doesn't make a difference whether she's there or not."

This bit of spontaneous silliness was all the ammunition Crystal needed to sail through the rest of the Oscar telecast. Throughout the rest of the night, there were Jack Palance jokes. Among other things, Crystal told the gala audience that Palance was backstage on a StairMaster, had just bungee jumped off the Hollywood sign, had rendezvoused with the space shuttle, and had fathered all the children in a jam-packed production number. The joke even extended into the next year's Academy Awards, when host Crystal made his entrance from atop a giant Oscar statue, towed through his teeth by Palance.

While it was all for laughs, Palance's oddball behavior led some to speculate that the actor, who passed away at 87 in 2006, had been drinking that evening.

What has any of this got to do with Marisa Tomei? It was presenter Palance who called the actress's name as the Best Supporting Actress winner. Soon after, a rumor spread that Palance either read Tomei's name by mistake or was too drunk to get it right and just read the last nominated actress's name on the TelePrompTer. The Academy of Motion Picture Arts and Sciences, embarrassed by the mix-up, just let the result stand.

Adding to the speculation was the general impression that Tomei was an outside shot at best in that category that year. *My Cousin Vinny* was a forgettable little comedy, and while Tomei was effective as Joe Pesci's abrasive love interest (Mona Lisa Vito), the one-time TV actress seemed outmatched by veteran film stars Miranda Richardson, Joan Plowright, Judy Davis, and Vanessa Redgrave.

An official at the Academy says, as a result of this rumor, Tomei's surprise win has been questioned countless times over the years. They point to the fact that two officials from the accounting firm of PriceWaterhouseCoopers are on stage at all times throughout the Oscar ceremony. If there ever was a mix-up such as the one suggested here, the officials would step up to the podium and correct it, says the Academy.

They also point out that, in order to prevent reporters and others from sneaking names off a script, the winner's names are never flashed on the

TelePrompTer. Instead, after the cue "and the Oscar goes to," presenters are prompted to look in the envelope and announce the winner.

As for how the rumor got started, a blind item in the *Hollywood Reporter* in March of 1994 suggested it was spread by the "former son-in-law of a distinguished Academy Award winner." Since that doesn't narrow it down very much, let's pin it on another culprit: film critic Rex Reed, who blabbed during a 1997 TV interview that he felt Palance was either "drunk" or "stoned" at the 1993 Oscar telecast and that Tomei's win was the result of a "massive cover-up."

Or perhaps slightly more than one-fifth of the Academy voters just loved her in *My Cousin Vinny* that year. The Academy insists that, in their nearly 80 year history, an Oscar has never been awarded by mistake.

In any event, maybe Tomei just wasn't supposed to win that supporting actress Oscar. When she moved in 2002, she temporarily misplaced the statue. Let's start a new rumor: Rex Reed stole it.

RUMOR: Entertainment Tonight's Mary Hart had her legs insured for $2 million dollars by Lloyd's of London.

TRUE: But just for a day. The publicity stunt was cooked up after a drastic set change at the long-running TV entertainment magazine resulted in a new desk that covered up Hart's fabulous pins.

Hart, a former Miss South Dakota, has been a fixture on the series since 1982. Calls and letters came flooding in to Paramount, the studio that produces the series. Hart's then-manager, star maker Jay Bernstein, got the bright idea to cash in on the fuss by taking out the one-day insurance policy, which, if my math is correct, worked out to $1 million a leg. Think of it as pin money. The stunt also led to a tidy endorsement deal with Hart showing off her gams clad in Hanes Hosiery.

The entertainment magazine quickly switched back to the see-through desk and even installed a special "leg light" to show off Hart's valuable assets.

There's another TV legend attached to Hart: that her voice once triggered epileptic seizures in a female viewer. This also, astonishingly, is true. The *New England Journal of Medicine* reported on the phenomenon in 1991. The quirky anecdote was picked up on by the producers of *Seinfeld*. An episode of the '90s sitcom finds Kramer (Michael Richards) thrown into convulsions whenever he hears Hart's perky voice. Maybe that explains Richards's racist and career-ending outburst at that comedy club...

CHAPTER 21

Smile When You Say That, Pardner: TV's Greatest Western Whoppers

Wyatt Earp, Jesse James, and Buffalo Bill weren't the only legends of the Wild West. By the end of the 1950s, there were 30 prime time westerns on TV screens, including *Gunsmoke, Wagon Train, Have Gun, Will Travel,* and *The Rifleman*—the numbers one through four shows during the 1958 to 1959 season. Seven westerns made the top-10 that year, with *Maverick* (number six), *Tales Of Wells Fargo* (number 7), and *The Life and Legend of Wyatt Earp* (number ten) also on the list.

Even before that, westerns were a staple of early television, although the first few were aimed strictly at kids. Shows like *Hopalong Cassidy, The Lone Ranger,* and *The Roy Rogers Show* were basically live action cartoons, some strung together from cheapie serial westerns shown in movie theaters on Saturday morning matinees.

I'll never forget encountering Clayton Moore, TV's original Lone Ranger, who played the cowboy hero from 1949 to 1957. (He died in 1999.) By the mid-80s, when he was still making public appearances in his powder blue cowboy suit and white Stetson, Moore seemed to believe he was the Lone Ranger. Sporting wraparound shades instead of a mask (the copyright holders ordered him to stop wearing it at one point as they shopped newer versions of the franchise), Moore startled critics by firing his six shooter into the air during an unforgettable press tour session. Fortunately for critics, Moore was shooting blanks!

I remember approaching the TV legend for a quote. "Are ya grindin'?" he asked, motioning toward my tape recorder. "Yes," I answered. "Shut 'er down," he snarled.

If the stars of the shows cannot tell fact from fiction, how are we supposed to cope?

The most popular western of them all, *Gunsmoke*, seems to have inspired the most myths and legends. Gather round, pardners, and listen to these strange tales from the dusty streets of Dodge City and beyond.

RUMOR: Before it was offered to James Arness, the part of Marshal Matt Dillon on Gunsmoke *was offered to John Wayne.*

UNSUBSTANTIATED: While The Simpsons *are closing in (in years if not in number of episodes),* Gunsmoke *remains the longest-running scripted series in American television, lasting 20 seasons and an incredible 635 episodes. The western ran from 1955 to 1975, with James Arness as straight-shooter Marshal Matt Dillon, setting the record as the actor who played the same role for the most consecutive years on one series. (Kelsey Grammer also played one character, Dr. Frasier Crane, for 20 consecutive years, but that was split over two series,* Cheers *and* Frasier.)

For baby boomers who grew up with the series, it is hard to imagine anyone other than Arness playing the tall, steadfast marshal of Dodge City. Still, the legend remains out there that, when it came time to cast the TV version of the radio drama, the producers' first choice was none other than the Duke himself, Mr. John Wayne.

The popular Web site TV Party suggests that CBS offered Wayne "a sweetheart deal with a two million dollar guarantee" to play Dillon, but that Wayne turned the offer down. The same notion is repeated in Tim Brooks and Earle Marsh's *The Complete Directory to Prime Time Network and Cable TV Shows* as well as *Entertainment Weekly*'s "The 100 Greatest TV Shows of All Time."

Yet this story was shot down like a Dodge City outlaw in the 1990 book, *Gunsmoke: A Complete History*, an exhaustive, episode-by-episode analysis of the series by authors Suzanne and Gabor Barabas. Asked about John Wayne and the part of Marshal Dillon, original *Gunsmoke* TV producer Charles Marquis Warren was quoted as saying, "It was never offered to him."

Warren, who died in 1990, should have known. A novelist specializing in western themes, he had branched out into screenwriting and directing when he was approached by CBS to help *Gunsmoke* make the transition from successful radio series to TV drama. He was also already well acquainted with Wayne, Hollywood's top cowboy star.

Like many other movie stars of the '50s, Wayne was wary of television. As one of the top box office draws of the day, he did appear on TV occasionally to promote his films, including a 1953 appearance on *The Milton Berle Show* and a well-publicized turn on *I Love Lucy*. But starring in his own series? Forget it, pilgrim.

While Warren would have loved to have had him as the star of his show, he says there was no way he would have seriously offered Wayne the Dillon part.

"One day when we were sitting in his bar I jokingly asked Wayne if he would consider doing Dillon," Warren told the Barabas. "He turned, grabbed me by the neck, and he took this triple-size martini and poured it on my head."

By 1955, Wayne would have known all about *Gunsmoke*. The series had been a hit on the radio for three years (eventually lasting nine seasons, ending its radio run in 1961). William Conrad—the future star of *Canon* as well as *Jake and the Fatman*—provided the deep, booming radio voice of Marshal Matt Dillon.

Conrad was reportedly the first choice of *Gunsmoke*'s radio producers to play the character on TV. But they weren't calling the shots on the video venture—Warren was. He and, presumably, CBS programmers deemed Conrad too tubby to play Dodge City's fastest draw.

Other actors were tested, including future Perry Mason star Raymond Burr (like Conrad, dismissed as too heavy), Denver Pyle, and Richard Boone, who would star a few years later in another popular adult western, *Have Gun Will Travel*.

How James Arness first came into the picture is a little murky. By several accounts, he was suggested to CBS and the producers by Wayne. That fits with the "don't take me, take the kid" scenario.

Arness, however, was already on Warren's radar. He directed the young Minnesota native in the 1952 prison drama *Hellgate*. When it came time to cast the TV western, Warren remembered two other actors from his film directing days: Milburn Stone (*Gunsmoke*'s cantankerous Doc), whom he directed in *Arrowhead* (1953), and Dennis Weaver (Dillon's limping sidekick Chester), directed by Warren in *Seven Angry Men* (1955).

At the time, Arness was a supporting player better known for his size (six foot seven) than his screen time. His best known credit before *Gunsmoke* was probably playing a monster in *The Thing from Another World*.

One person who did know him well was John Wayne. Three years before *Gunsmoke*, Arness landed a contract job working for Wayne's film production company, where he supported the movie star in films like *Big Jim McLain* and *Island in the Sky*.

Arness has said many times that Wayne not only recommended him for the role of Matt Dillon but also talked him into taking it. According to commentary on the *Gunsmoke* 50th Anniversary volume one DVD of the series, Arness was auditioned and offered the part just weeks before shooting on the series commenced. With his movie career inching forward, the then 32-year-old actor was on the fence about television. He consulted a director pal and then Wayne himself about the move. The director said don't do it, it will derail your movie career. Wayne had a completely different take on the opportunity. Recalling his own early days grinding out dozens of quickie Saturday morning matinees and serials, he urged Arness to play the TV marshal, suggesting the experience would make him a better actor and horseman. Plus, "The whole world will get to know you," was Wayne's advice as Arness recalls it. "He talked me into it, and thank God he did."

As a favor to his buddy Warren—or maybe as a way for making up for that martini dunking—Wayne went so far as to shoot a special introduction for *Gunsmoke*, which premiered on September 10, 1955. Standing on a western set in full cowboy regalia, Wayne gave the show a ringing endorsement. "No, I'm not in it," he said. "I wish I were, though, because I think it's the best thing of its kind that's come along. I hope you'll agree with me."

Viewers did agree. In less than two years, *Gunsmoke* was the number one show on television and stayed on top of the ratings for four straight seasons. It opened the door for a flood of similar adult westerns. By the end of the '50s, there were 30 "oaters" on the three networks.

Continuing his intro, Wayne went even further in his praise for Arness. "When I first heard about the show *Gunsmoke*, I knew there was only one man to play in it. James Arness. He's a young fella, maybe new to some of you, but I've worked with him and I predict he'll be a big star. So you may as well get used to him like you've had to get used to me. And now I'm proud to present my friend Jim Arness in *Gunsmoke*."

The cast and crew gathered at Arness's house to watch that first episode were blown away by Wayne's gesture of support. "All of us were tremendously surprised to see Duke Wayne do that intro because none of us knew it was coming," Arness says on the DVD commentary to the first episode.

The fact that Wayne did that intro has probably added to the legend that he was offered the part first and turned it down. Maybe he was offered the part, although Warren insisted it was only a half-joking gesture. Even if CBS did tempt him with a two million dollar offer, there can be no doubt that Wayne was never interested in playing Dillon. His movie career was thriving and TV was still seen as a humbling step down for any Hollywood leading man.

Wayne and Arness do have one other thing in common—their birthday. Both were born on May 26, although Wayne was born in 1907, Arness in 1923.

RUMOR: *Dennis Weaver (Chester) limped on* Gunsmoke *to draw attention away from James Arness's wooden leg.*

FALSE: *Somebody was pulling Arness's leg with this rumor, although it almost could have been true.*

Long before he saddled up for *Gunsmoke*, Arness served in the United States Army. His great height (six foot seven) was put to the test during World War II at the Battle of Anzio, where he was reportedly used to gauge the deepness of the water by being the first off his unit's landing craft.

Arness was cut down by German machine gun fire at that battle and spent nearly a year in the hospital recovering from severe wounds to his leg and knee. He was discharged from the army with a bronze medal and a purple heart and walked with a slight limp for the rest of his life.

What he didn't have was a wooden leg. In fact, Arness's leg eventually grew sturdy enough for him to indulge in one of his favorite pastimes: surfing.

The character of Chester Goode was not described as having a physical handicap on the original radio version of *Gunsmoke*. So why did Dennis Weaver have such a pronounced limp on TV? Weaver had no such limitation in real life, having excelled as an athlete at the University of Oklahoma. He also finished sixth in the decathlon trials while trying out for the 1948 U.S. Olympic team.

As Weaver, who died in 2006, explained in the commentary to volume one of the *Gunsmoke* 50th Anniversary DVD, Chester's limp came about after a suggestion from the producer, Charles Warren. Most sidekicks were "too old or too fast or too something to get involved in the physical stuff," Warren suggested to Weaver. He wanted Chester to be a nonviolent character who nevertheless had a reason to always be hanging around Marshal Dillon's digs.

Weaver went home and worked on a stiff-legged limp. "I hopped around the backyard for a couple of days over boxes and it seemed to work," he said.

Arness said that Chester's bum leg gave Weaver "an outstanding individuality with that character." He also points out that it was the first time a main character on a TV show had any kind of a physical disability.

Since Weaver, several other actors in prime time series have affected a limp to help flesh out their character, including two doctors—*ER*'s Kerry Weaver (Laura Innes) and *House*'s cranky MD, Dr. Gregory House (Hugh Laurie).

The limp wasn't always so easy to live with, Weaver conceded. While riding a horse was no problem, "Did you ever try to build a camp fire stiff-legged?" he asks on the DVD. Weaver had to take yoga to work out some of the kinks.

An added feature on the *Gunsmoke* DVD shows Weaver guesting on *The Ed Sullivan Show* in 1958. Appearing in character as Chester, he hopped around obstacles set up on the stage to demonstrate how Chester could still scissor-leap over trouble. Unfortunately, Weaver's "lame" leg caught the first fence and he landed on his kisser.

Weaver stuck with *Gunsmoke* through the first six seasons and then appeared occasionally for three more when the western expanded from a half-hour to an hour-long show. He left the series for good in 1964.

"If I had known at the time that I was going to be walking stiff-legged for nine years," said Weaver, "I might have had a different thought about it."

RUMOR: *Albert Einstein once appeared as a guest star on* Gunsmoke.

FALSE: *You don't have to be a genius to figure out that this rumor was a fake.*

For one thing, and this is a biggie, even for a world-renowned physicist, Einstein died on April 18, 1955, five months before *Gunsmoke* premiered.

It's possible that the father of the theory of relativity could have been booked onto the earlier radio version of the series, which began in 1952, but his thick German accent would have sounded a little out of place at the Longhorn Saloon.

How did this crazy rumor get started? It seems to date back to 1993, when another renowned physicist, Stephen Hawking, guest starred on *Star Trek: The Next Generation*. Brent Spiner, who played yellow-eyed droid Data on the sci-fi series, was quoted at the time saying Hawking's cameo was "the most notable moment in television history since Albert Einstein guest starred on *Gunsmoke*."

In other words, E (Einstein) equals M (myth) times C (crazy) squared.

RUMOR: *There were lyrics to the* Bonanza *theme.*

TRUE: *Lorne Greene, who played Pa Cartwright for 13 seasons on the popular western, once had a hit recording in the early '60s with a western-themed song* called "Ringo." Nicknamed the "Voice of Doom" in Canada for his World War II radio broadcasts, Greene's rich baritone could really belt out a song, even if he was more of a dramatic reader than a singer.

So it should come as no surprise then to learn that there exists a recording of Greene singing the Bonanza theme song, familiar to fans of the western as a strictly orchestral score.

The Canadian-born actor sings the Bonanza theme on an album titled Lorne Greene and the Western Classics: On the Ponderosa. He also sang it, along with costars Dan Blocker (Hoss), Pernell Roberts (Adam), and Little Joe (Michael Landon), in an alternate opening to the series that was filmed but never used. The clip, which wound up in a 1991 Landon tribute special (the actor died of liver cancer that same year), shows the Cartwright clan riding up on horseback, singing their heads off.

The memory of that day made Landon laugh out loud when I asked him about it in March of 1991 (just two weeks before his cancer diagnosis). At the time, the resilient TV star was just prepping his fourth series, the CBS drama Us. Not yet aware of just how sick he was, Landon was friendly and accommodating and bursting with stories about the bad old Bonanza days.

Landon recalled the day that singing intro was shot and how ridiculous they all felt doing it. "We nearly fell off our horses from laughing so hard," he said.

Thankfully, somebody realized that the sight of four Cartwrights singing on horseback at the start of the show every week was just too hilarious. A simple orchestral version of the opening, complete with the searing iron and the flaming map, became Bonanza's signature starting point.

Landon, who starred in three straight hits, including Little House on the Prairie and Highway to Heaven, said he was only 21 when he started working on Bonanza. Looking at episodes 30 years later sometimes made him wince. "The first two years, I wore a hat that looked like a yarmulke—the itty-bitty cowboy hat," he said.

He used to kid Greene about his horsemanship. "The way he talked before the show started, I thought he was a Mountie," said Landon. "The first day we ride—I'm riding behind him—he'd come off that horse so high I could have shot bad guys underneath him!"

As much as he tried to forget them, Landon still recalled some of the lyrics to the Bonanza theme and belted them out that day in his office. The words and music to the theme were by Ray Evans and Jay Livingston.

CHAPTER 22

Super Lie: A Rumor That Spread Faster Than a Speeding Bullet

RUMOR: George Reeves, the actor who portrayed Superman on television in the '50s, believed he had acquired the character's super powers and accidentally killed himself by jumping out a window and trying to fly or by trying to stop a bullet.

FALSE: The 1959 headline stung like a bolt of kryptonite to the head: "TV's 'Superman' Kills Self".

That's how it read on the entire front page of the *New York Post* after George Reeves, who had come to embody the "Man of Steel" on *The Adventures of Superman* (1952–57), was found dead in his Beverly Hills home of a gun shot wound to the head.

Reeves's blood alcohol count was about two and a half times over the legal limit at the time of his death. While no note was ever found, the official coroner's report concluded that it was suicide.

Yet, nearly 50 years later, the circumstances seem as suspicious as ever. Among the puzzlers at the scene: no fingerprints were found on the gun; no powder burns were found on the head wound (indicating it might not have been fired from close range); two bullet holes were found on the floor of his bedroom; and Reeves's three guests at the time, including his fiancée Leonore Lemon (who left California the next week—never to return), took 45 minutes after the shooting to call the police.

Exploring whether or not Reeves's death was a murder or a suicide isn't the purpose of this book. (There are several other books that go into great detail about that, including *Speeding Bullet: The Life and Bizarre Death of George Reeves* by Jan Alan Henderson.) But some background is needed to understand how all the "Superman is dead" rumors were spread.

Reeves' sensational death has been explored on TV on everything from *Unsolved Mysteries* to *20/20*. Early in 2000, A&E's *Biography* series examined it during something they called "Foul Play Week," with the focus on five of Hollywood's most lurid true-life tales. It also inspired a full length feature film, *Hollywoodland* (2006), starring Ben Affleck as Reeves.

For years, stories circulated throughout schoolyards that a depressed Reeves, down about being typecast, wanted to prove that he wasn't "faster than a speeding bullet" by shooting himself in the head or jumping out a window. The general assumption was that he was depressed over the state of his career. That *Superman* had been canceled and he was out of work. That he was hopelessly typecast and no future TV work was on the horizon. None of that, apparently, was completely true. Reeves's friends said he was in high spirits after main sponsor Kellogg's confirmed a new, 26-episode season would commence shooting that September. (The series ran for six seasons and 104 episodes.) Besides his dual role as Superman/Clark Kent, Reeves, 45, was set to direct several episodes and saw that as a way to extend his Hollywood career. (He had already directed the last three episodes of the series.) Reeves was also excited about marrying new sweetheart Leonore Lemmon, an event that was, according to some reports, set to take place in Mexico just three days later. Europe was booked for the honeymoon.

Instead, in the early hours of June 16th, Reeves was found dead upstairs in his house. While Lemon remains a prime suspect for many conspiracy buffs, some still point the finger at Reeves's jilted lover, Toni Mannix, a former mob moll who was married to a powerful MGM studio executive. Mannix had been reportedly calling Reeves 20 times a day and had badgered mutual friends, including original series' Lois Lane, Phyllis Coates, to break off his engagement to Lemmon.

Mannix had every right to be jealous. Reeves and Lemmon were living in a house Mannix had bought for him. Her husband allegedly had connections to the mob. Did she order a hit on the Man of Steel? In 1987, when I first asked Jack Larson (who played cub reporter Jimmy Olsen on *The Adventures of Superman*) about Reeves's death, he was convinced that foul play was involved. "George wasn't depressed, he was excited," Larson said. "The series was picked up for another two seasons, and he was really looking forward to getting back to work." By 2004, however, when I spoke with him again at a Los Angeles launch of *The Adventures of Superman* on

DVD, Larson had come around to accepting the official report that Reeves had committed suicide. In any event, Larson said he was "permanently saddened by George's death."

So were a lot of adoring kids who used to run around their parent's yards with dish towels tied around their necks as capes who just could not believe the news. Like the John F. Kennedy assassination four years later, or former Beatle John Lennon's 1980 murder, this was a death that went far beyond the passing of a famous person. Reeves's shocking suicide was like a death in the family. Beyond that, for young fans of the series, Superman was supposed to be invincible. How could he have died, let alone take his own life?

Judging by comments from now fifty-something fans on several *Superman* and Reeves tribute sites, some parents consoled their youngsters by altering the facts. Some might have also been trying to sneak in a lesson about jumping out of trees or any other copycat super-stunts their kids might be contemplating. Telling their kids that the actor who played Superman died from jumping out a window was a sure way to get Junior's attention and scare some sense into the lad. The misinformation grew into rumor and legend.

The rumors also stemmed from the fact that it would have seemed impossible for this tremendous father figure to have taken his own life. Reeves was adored by kids, both on TV and in his many personal appearances in costume as Superman. By all reports, he was very conscious of his image and how it had to be projected to kids. It would have been hard to accept that such a hero and role model committed suicide.

In a 1954 *TV Guide* cover story (one of the most valuable and collectable *TV Guide* covers, fetching in excess of $1,000 from collectors), Reeves said he had given up smoking, "Believing that Superman should never be seen with a cigarette." The article also described Reeves as "a thoroughly likable man with a ready grin, a keen sense of humor, and no illusions about his importance in the TV hierarchy."

While Reeves was always careful to project respect for the role and his young fans, there were other reports that he was not always that thrilled to be typecast as the Man of Steel. He reportedly saw the role as a giant comedown from a career that began as an extra on one of Hollywood's all-time great pictures, *Gone with the Wind*. Reeves's promising career was sidetracked by a stint in the army during World War II. When he returned to Hollywood, his career momentum seemed stalled. He was apparently talked into accepting the Superman role by his agent who assured him that the low-budget production would probably never see the light of day.

Instead, the widely syndicated series was an international success, playing in two dozen countries in several languages. Did the role typecast him? Absolutely. Reeves was all but cut out of *From Here to Eternity* after preview audiences howled "Hey, Superman!" every time he took the screen. Was his career on the skids? Despite a bad back, Reeves was apparently contemplating taking up wrestling to tide himself over until the next Superman season arrived. He was scheduled to box light heavyweight champion Archie Moore the day after his tragic death. That probably was a sobering career move for a guy who once worked with the likes of Clark Gable and Claudette Colbert.

Just a few months earlier, Reeves had also been injured in a car crash, suffering a concussion. He was on painkillers and other medication. Mix in too much booze and you don't have to be *Daily Planet* reporter Clark Kent to see that Reeves was probably not his Super self on the night of June 15, 1959.

Still, what a shame and what a waste. Who wouldn't have wanted a happy ending for this handsome, well-liked actor who lucked into the role of a lifetime, even if it inadvertently may have also contributed to his death?

CHAPTER 23

Stars on Ice: Stars Who Supposedly Died on Television

Nothing kills a career on TV like death—especially if you die on TV. But how often does that happen? More often than you'd think, or at least there have been several people who have died while making TV.

Crocodile Hunter Steve Irwin was a recent, tragic example. The 44-year-old Australian adventurer was killed in September of 2006, not by one of the thousands of crocodiles or deadly snakes he had wrangled over the years, but by a manta ray that speared him through the heart with its barbed tail during a routine dive. Irwin was shooting scenes for a children's series he was producing at the time.

Other stars, such as John Ritter and Jon-Erik Hexum, died or became fatally ill while on TV sound stages. Ritter, best known for his slapstick antics back in the '70s while playing bachelor Jack Tripper on *Three's Company*, died after his aorta ruptured during rehearsals for his new sitcom, *8 Simple Rules*. He had seemingly been in perfect health and even better spirits.

Hexum accidentally shot himself in the head with a prop gun while on the set of his 1984 action adventure series *Cover Up*. The tragedy led to stricter guidelines for firearms on sound stages.

In 1991, about a month after the premiere of his new series, *The Royal Family*, Redd Foxx—who was always clutching his heart and claiming this was "the big one, Elizabeth," in the '70s on *Sanford and Son*—had a massive heart attack and died. He was on a sound stage, rehearsing scenes from his new series.

One of Hollywood's biggest stars, Orson Welles, did not die on TV, but did tape a memorable episode of *The Merv Griffin Show* on the last day of his life. On October 9, 1985, at age 70, Welles sat with his old pal Griffin, opened up about his up and down career, spoke of former loves Rita Hayworth and Marlene Dietrich, and even performed an elaborate magic trick for the audience. Then he went out to dinner at his favorite spot, Ma Maison, went home, and died. He was found next to his typewriter and apparently died at the keys. All that was missing was for the last word he typed to have been "Rosebud."

These real life tragedies have probably led to rumors about other deaths on Hollywood sets. Some are sad, some less serious, and others a little shocking—mainly because they actually happened.

RUMOR: Back in the '50s, Brazilian Bombshell Carmen Miranda had a heart attack and died during a live performance opposite Jimmy Durante on The Texaco Star Theater.

PARTIALLY TRUE: The singer with the tutti-frutti 'do was born Maria do Carmo Miranda da Cunha in Portugal. She was nicknamed "Carmen" by her father, an opera fan who adored Bizet.

By the time she was one, her family moved to Brazil. She became a singer, dancer, and actress. Her career took off during World War II when European markets were closed to American film exhibitors. Suddenly Mexico and Latin America were in vogue and Miranda samba-d her way to fame. She was Brazil's highest-paid entertainer throughout the war, banking $200,000 in 1945 alone.

Still, all that fruit piled a mile high on her trademark tutti-frutti hats weighed her down. Many at home saw her as a Yankee sellout. She felt alienated from her homeland, boycotting Brazil for 14 years.

The tension may have contributed to a drug habit; Miranda was eventually hooked on amphetamines and barbiturates in addition to booze and cigarettes. (But not cocaine as was alleged in Kenneth Anger's muckraking scandal tome, *Hollywood Babylon*.)

All of her vices took their toll on the night of August 4, 1955. That was when she made her final appearance on *The Texaco Star Theater*, hosted by Jimmy Durante. Kinescoped footage of the fateful night was shown on an episode of A&E's *Biography* series. It showed the usually sure-footed Miranda stumbling and faltering during a lively dance number. Trooper Durante joked about it and held her up by the end. Miranda somehow managed to summon the fortitude to smile, wave, and walk off stage one last time.

What she and the others on the show didn't know was that she had suffered a heart attack. Later that night, she died at her Beverly Hills home. She was 46.

RUMOR: *A guest on* The Dick Cavett Show *died right in the middle of a taping.*

TRUE: *Here's one you couldn't make up. Jerome Rodale, a 72-year-old author and longevity expert (among his enterprises was the magazine* Prevention*), really thought he had all the time in the world. "I'm going to live to be 100 unless I'm run down by a sugar-crazed taxi driver," he declared in a 1971* New York Times Magazine *article.*

On June 5, 1971—the day after that article came out—Rodale was a guest at a taping of *The Dick Cavett Show* (1968–73). Originally a daytime show, this late night ABC talk show was billed as the "hip" alternative to *The Tonight Show Starring Johnny Carson* in the late '60s/early '70s.

As their 30-minute chat ended, Cavett turned his attention to his next guest, journalist Pete Hamill. Suddenly, Rodale's head slumped to his chest and he let out what sounded like a snore.

Talking about the incident in 2007, Cavett recalled that the sudden noise actually "got a laugh." Rodale had proven to be a pretty funny guest up to that point.

So Cavett was typically irreverent in the moment. "Are we boring you, Mr. Rodale?" he asked. No response. The talk show host went over to take Rodale's pulse. There wasn't one.

Two interns who just happened to be in the studio audience rushed the stage, but it was too late. Rodale had suffered a massive coronary.

"Forty times a year, at least," Cavett told me, "someone comes up and says, 'I'll never forget the look on your face when that guy died.'"

"How? Were you in the studio?" Cavett inevitably asks.

The episode never aired. The taping wrapped about two hours before air time and the decision was quickly made to pull the show. "It never occurred to anybody [to air it], it was so awful," said Cavett. "How would you put it on television?"

The following night, Cavett explained to the studio audience and viewers at home exactly what happened. That's probably why many people think they actually saw Rodale die on *The Dick Cavett Show*. The unaired episode was not included in any of the DVD boxed sets of *The Dick Cavett Show* released in 2006. Cavett says he has the master tape locked in his house, where it will remain.

The only reason it exists at all was because Marshall Brickman—who would go on to collaborate with Woody Allen on *Annie Hall* and other film scripts—happened to be in the control room that night. Brickman was working for Cavett at the time and overturned the director's order to cut. Cavett, who has only watched the scene once—about a month after it occurred—says the whole thing is on tape, "From the couch to the floor."

The shock for Cavett was rehearing some of the things Rodale said in the last half hour of his life. "None of us remembered that he had said, 'I plan to live to be a hundred,' and, another time, 'I never felt better in my life.'" Rodale also boasted, according to Cavett, that he had recently tumbled down a flight of stairs "and laughed all the way to the bottom."

It is possible that a bootleg of the tape is still out there. Cavett had heard that a few engineers who were working the show "ran off a tape that night to scare their girlfriends."

One footnote: Cavett also had the last interview with Jimi Hendrix, taped just days before the guitar god died of a drug overdose.

RUMOR: Pinky Lee collapsed and died on the set of his '50s children's series.

FALSE: If you can sing the words to The Pinky Lee Show *theme song ("Yoo-hoo it's me/My name is Pinky Lee/I skip and run with lots of fun/For every he and she..."), congratulations...you're old!*

The somewhat forgotten children's entertainer was the Pee-Wee Herman of the '50s. Dressed in his trademark plaid hat and suit, he would lisp ditties, read storybooks, skip around his set, and just generally almost explode with energy. Paired with Howdy Doody on NBC in the mid-50s, he was a hit with kids, if loathed by parents and critics.

On September 20, 1955, during a live broadcast, he collapsed. At first it was feared that Lee had suffered a heart attack, but his condition was later diagnosed as a severe sinus infection. Doctors ordered him to rest for a year. His show continued for a while without him, but when he was finally healthy enough to return to TV in 1957, he was reassigned to emcee *The Gumby Show*. Suddenly he was playing second banana to a little green ball of clay.

When that didn't last, Lee had a hard time finding other work. Broadcasters seemed terrified that the burlesque clown might collapse again on their network. He tried a few comebacks, notably on a short-lived '60s series. He died at 86 in 1993—of a heart attack.

RUMOR: *The cast of '60s sitcom* Green Acres *ate Arnold the Pig after the show's final episode.*

FALSE: *"Green Acres was the place to be" blared the catchy and familiar theme song. But was it if you were a pig?*

The '60s sitcom was one of several rural comedies on CBS at the time. *The Beverly Hillbillies* and *Petticoat Junction* were also very popular and occasionally featured interconnected storylines. Middle America just couldn't get enough of, say, Mr. Drucker. Eddie Albert and Eva Gabor were the stars, playing former Manhattan socialites who were fishes out of water in farm hamlet Hooterville. Among their new neighbors were Fred and Doris Ziffel and their pet pig Arnold, a precocious porker they treated like their first born. According to *Green Acres* resident pig wrangler Frank Inn, there were up to 12 different pigs used in the role of Arnold Ziffel on the show. None of them was ever eaten.

The delicious rumor apparently spread when one of the cast members joked to a reporter that they pigged out on Arnold at the show's farewell barbecue. Stars Edward Arnold and Eva Gabor denied this story several times. "It's baloney!" said Arnold, who must have meant to say ham.

Appendix

LAW AND ORDER: TERMS AND DEFINITIONS

Not everything in this book is, strictly speaking, a rumor, even though that is how the various stories are all framed. I've just used the word "rumor" in a general way to represent the various legends, myths, hoaxes, and strange but true tales found on these pages.

For the record—along with examples from the book—here are dictionary definitions of all of those terms. Like suntan lotion, they should be applied when needed:

Apocryphal. *adj.* Of questionable authorship or authenticity. Erroneous; fictitious. *Mikey, the kid from those Life cereal spots, died from eating Pop Rocks and drinking soda.*

Doozy. *n. Slang.* Something extraordinary or bizarre. *The cast of '60s' sitcom* Green Acres *ate Arnold the Pig after the show's final episode.*

Fable. *n.* A story about legendary persons and exploits. A falsehood; a lie. *Radio transmissions picked up on Lucille Ball's dental fillings led to the capture of Japanese spies.*

Fallacy. *n., pl.* -cies. A false notion. A statement or an argument based on a false or invalid inference. Incorrectness of reasoning or belief; erroneousness. *TV's first interracial kiss was between Captain James T. Kirk and Lieutenant Uhura on* Star Trek.

Gossip. *n.* Rumor or talk of a personal, sensational, or intimate nature. *Ernie and Bert are gay and will soon marry on* Sesame Street.

Hoax. *n.* An act intended to deceive or trick. Something that has been established or accepted by fraudulent means. *Adam Rich, who played adorable tyke Nicholas on the '70s drama* Eight Is Enough, *was murdered in the '90s by a desperate, out-of-work Los Angeles stagehand.*

Myth. *n.* A popular belief or story that has become associated with a person, institution, or occurrence, especially one considered to illustrate a cultural ideal. *George Reeves, the actor who portrayed Superman on television in the '50s, believed he had acquired the character's super powers and accidentally killed himself by trying to fly.*

Publicity stunt. *n.* A planned event designed to attract the public's attention to the promoters or their causes. Entertainment Tonight's *Mary Hart had her legs insured for $2 million dollars by Lloyd's of London.*

Rumor. *n.* A piece of unverified information of uncertain origin usually spread by word of mouth. Unverified information received from another; hearsay. *Ken Osmond, who played Wally's creepy pal Eddie Haskell on* Leave It to Beaver, *grew up to become the notorious porn star John Holmes.*

Tall tale. *n.* An entertaining and often oral account of a real or fictitious occurrence. An untrue declaration. *Jim Nabors married Rock Hudson.*

Untruth. *n.* Something untrue; a lie. The condition of being false; lack of truth. *Tommy Hilfiger made racist statements about African Americans, Hispanics, and Asians on* Oprah Winfrey *and was tossed off the show.*

Urban legend. *n.* An apocryphal story involving incidents of the recent past, often including elements of humor and horror, that spreads quickly and is popularly believed to be true. *The wife of a famous golfer was once a guest on* The Tonight Show. *Carson asked if she did anything special for her hubby before a big tournament for good luck. Her reply: "I kiss his balls." Said Carson, "That must make his putter stick out."*

Whopper. *n.* Slang. A gross untruth. *Josh Saviano, the geeky best friend from* The Wonder Years, *grew up to become Marilyn Manson.*

Index

About the Author

BILL BRIOUX served for two years as the Los Angeles bureau chief for the Canadian edition of *TV Guide*. He has written *The Toronto Sun*'s daily television column since 1999, winning two Edward A. Dunlop Awards for critical writing. Besides *TV Guide* and *The Toronto Sun*, his articles on television have appeared in *The Toronto Star*, *The Globe & Mail*, *Starweek*, and *TVTimes* magazines. Bill Brioux is currently on the board of directors of the Television Critics Association.